ONE
CHURCH,
MANY
CONGREGATIONS

Ministry for the Third Millennium
Edited by Lyle E. Schaller

ONE CHURCH, MANY CONGREGATIONS

The Key Church Strategy

J V THOMAS
J. TIMOTHY AHLEN

ABINGDON PRESS / Nashville

ONE CHURCH, MANY CONGREGATIONS
THE KEY CHURCH STRATEGY

Copyright © 1999 by Abingdon Press

This book is printed on acid-free paper.

Library of Congress Cataloging-in-Publication Data

Thomas, J V, 1931-
   One church, many congregations : the Key Church Strategy / J V Thomas, J. Timothy Ahlen.
      p.   cm.—(Ministry for the third millennium)
   ISBN 0-687-08599-3 (alk. paper)
   1. Church growth.   2. Church development, New.   3. New Church Strategy (Program)
I. Ahlen, J. Timothy, 1953-   .   II. Title.   III. Series.
BV652.25.T46   1999
253—dc21   99-21484
                                                                            CIP

99 00 01 02 03 04 05 06 07 08—10 9 8 7 6 5 4 3 2 1

MANUFACTURED IN THE UNITED STATES OF AMERICA

To Bob Bull and Jim Brunk

CONTENTS

ACKNOWLEDGMENTS

To recite the names of all the people to whom the authors are indebted would take as many pages as the book's text, so we will not attempt to name them all. However, both of us are indebted to our wives, Lucy Thomas and Lynda Ahlen, for their patience with us as we have toiled on this project.

We also want to express our gratitude to Bob and Gelene Bull, who have served as J V's right hands for the past five years. Charles Chaney and Larry Lewis have been instrumental in the development of the Key Church into a National Strategy. Other great missions strategists, pastors, and ministers of missions have contributed ideas, inspiration, and guidance as the Key Church strategy has unfolded.

Most of all we thank God for allowing us to be a small part of his Kingdom.

J V Thomas
Tim Ahlen

FOREWORD

The past several decades have brought an unprecedented quantity of research, reflections, insights, experiments, and observations on the state of American Christianity in general and on evangelism and church growth in particular.

What have we learned?

High on the list of learnings, we have discovered that the most effective—and often the lowest cost—way to reach new generations of American-born residents and recent immigrants with the gospel of Jesus Christ is through new worshiping communities. The book of Acts tells us this really is not a new insight, but was a key to the growth of the Christian church in the first century.

Second, we have rediscovered the influence of the cultural context and the importance of indigenous leadership. While cross-cultural leadership can be valuable, it requires a far higher level of skill than is required of indigenous leaders. This point is movingly made at the end of chapter 4 when Virginia is asked to officiate at a funeral service.

A third lesson is that we are not all completely convinced of the best way to plant new missions to reach new generations and recent immigrants. In the post–Civil War era, tens of thousands of existing congregations accepted the responsibility to start new missions. In the 1950s, however, there was widespread agreement that this task could be accomplished most effectively by and through denominational systems. By the end of the 1970s, many of the mainline denominations had moved new church development to a relatively low place on their agendas. The vast majority of new worshiping communities launched in the 1990s are being started by (1) entrepreneurial individuals, (2) existing congregations, (3) a combination of those two, or (4) completely independently by three to seven laypersons.

Fourth, while this is still in dispute, a growing body of evidence supports the contention that by the twentieth year of a new mission's existence, most of them have placed taking care of the current membership far higher on their list of priorities than reaching unchurched people.

One part of the explanation for this is culture, rather than their place of residence, is the crucial reference point for self-identification by a growing proportion of the American population. One example of this is the congregation meeting in a building near the university dormitories rarely reaches as many as fifty dorm residents. A second example is the Anglo congregation founded in a new Anglo residential community in 1948. Forty years later, the Anglo congregation is growing older and smaller as American-born blacks or Latinos or recent immigrants from southeast Asia move in after the Anglos move away. A third example is today's congregation composed largely of adults in the forty-five to sixty age cohort that is unable to reach those who are eighteen to twenty-three years old.

A fifth learning, which also is a point of dispute, is that long-term financial subsidies can be one of the most effective tools for undermining the health, vitality, and institutional strength of a congregation. The Episcopal Church may be the leader in both documenting and acting on this conclusion. In other religious traditions, long-term financial subsidies have evolved into an untouchable entitlement.

A sixth learning is that the road to health and vitality in congregational life includes designing the organizational structure around missions rather than governance.

A seventh, and perhaps the most important learning in the churches in this century, is that Christianity is a transformational religion, and one of the responsibilities of worshiping communities is to facilitate the transformation of believers into disciples.

An eighth learning is that the most useful synonym for "church" is not a "building," but rather a "collection of believers." That expanded definition of the word "church" helps people understand that one church can consist of five or ten or twenty or two hundred different worshiping communities meeting in many different places. When church is defined as people rather than as real estate, the ceiling on creativity is raised several notches.

These eight learnings are major themes in this book. These eight learnings also represent the foundation on which the Key Church Strategy has been built.

A ninth learning, on which there also is less than universal agreement, explains why we invited two Southern Baptists from Texas to write a book to be published by The United Methodist Publishing House.

All across the North American continent and beyond is a growing conviction that Christians can learn from one another. Christians in the United States can learn from Christians in Korea or in Canada or in Russia. Lutherans can learn from Episcopalians. Presbyterians can learn from what the independent churches are doing. Methodists can learn from Mennonites.

These two Texans have spent most of the last twenty years inventing, practicing, reflecting on, refining, testing, teaching, propagating, documenting, and building the philosophical, theological, and organizational framework for an exciting and effective strategy for evangelism. It can be adapted to fit the congregation averaging three hundred and fifty at worship or the congregation averaging thirty-five at worship or the one averaging thirty-five hundred at worship. It is a high-commitment strategy. It is, in financial terms, a very low-cost strategy. It can be adapted to fit the culture of your congregation and the location of your principal meeting place.

To be more precise, this book has been written to share what I believe is one of the most innovative, practical, and effective approaches to outreach ministries I have encountered in nearly four decades of working with congregations. The basic concept is now being practiced by United Methodists in Indiana, by Lutherans in North Dakota, and by scores of other congregations in other places.

In simple terms, it boils down to the discovery that one congregation can meet in two different locations. One example is the Global Mission Church with two meeting places—one in Silver Spring, Maryland, and the other in Seoul, Korea. Several more modest-scale examples are described in this book.

The central thesis, however, is that instead of placing 100 percent of the responsibility on others to come to our meeting place, this strategy calls for us to carry the gospel of Jesus Christ to other people on their turf.

This has turned out to be an effective strategy to enable one relatively homogeneous congregation to cross the barriers of social class, culture, language, race, nationality, geography, age, and education.

Two of the central components of this strategy are (1) going to where the people are rather than waiting for them to come to what they often perceive as an intimidating building housing people who "are not like us," and (2) cultivating, encouraging, and trusting indigenous leadership.

A third component of the larger strategy, however, is frequently overlooked. This is the time, energy, patience, conversations, and persuasion that are usually required before the leaders of a congregation will venture forth to implement the Key Church Strategy. It is a relatively simple act to hand someone a book and suggest,"Read this and adapt that strategy to fit your situation."

This introduces the one serious reservation about the Key Church Strategy. Who will introduce it into your congregation? A staff member from your regional judicatory? Your pastor? A new member who moved here after serving as a volunteer in implementing this strategy for several years in another congregation? Your missions committee? Three to five laypersons who spent a couple of days visiting and studying the implementation of this strategy in another congregation? The governing board of your congregation? Someone from the national home missions board of your denomination? That newly arrived minister of missions on your staff who introduced and helped to implement the Key Church Strategy in another congregation? Your Long Range Planning Committee? The women's organization in your church? A visiting pastor or minister of missions in a congregation that began to implement this strategy three or four years ago? The group from your congregation who spent three days at a workshop offered by a teaching church that included an introduction to off-campus ministries? One deeply committed, determined, patient, tenacious, and mission-driven member of your congregation who has read this book? An influential and persistent leader in your congregation who is convinced "No" means "Let's talk about it some more before we decide to do it."

The best answer may be at least five or six of the above.

Do you want to see your congregation become a multicultural parish that includes people from a variety of cultural, nationality, income, educational, occupational, and social class categories?

Or is your top priority to find a way to challenge the believers in your church to be transformed into deeply committed disciples of Jesus Christ?

The Key Church Strategy can be the way to accomplish both of those goals.

Lyle E. Schaller
Naperville, Illinois

INTRODUCTION

Some of the adults at the Creek Point Apartments had been involved in church life in the past. Most of them had been out of church for years when Nancy and Jerry Sayers burst onto the scene. They wanted to start a church—right on the apartment property—and they wanted the residents to make up the congregation. At first a little suspicious, the residents declined to participate. When Jerry and Nancy kept showing up week after week, the residents finally thought there might be some substance to these crazy church folks. Relationships developed and it was not long before a congregation of fifteen to twenty adults was meeting weekly for Bible study and worship. The only public meeting place was the manager's office. Every Sunday, the apartment residents wandered over, sat down, and worshiped God.

When the congregation had been meeting for about six months or so, it finally dawned on its members that they were a church. A couple of the older members observed that if the group really was a church, they needed to start taking up an offering. The rest of the congregation agreed, so the next Sunday they all came prepared to give an offering. At the end of the sermon, the preacher passed a hat and, one by one, the members of the tiny congregation placed their money inside. When the service was over they all circled around the hat and looked with pride on the $4.51 they had collected. One of the younger members asked, "Well, now that we have it, what are we going to do with it?" A wise old gentleman, standing back from the circle replied, "I suggest we give it all away to a church that really needs it!" And so they gave their offering to a small, inner-city congregation up the road.

In another section of the same city, a small church had started in a predominantly Hispanic community of duplexes and fourplexes. The owner of the rental community had donated one of the duplexes to the poor congregation so they would have a place to hold services. Three rooms, the largest of which was the fifteen-by-fifteen-foot living room, served well for the first two months. By then, all three rooms were filled with more than forty people in average attendance. Pastor Ben Lopez began looking for another place to meet, but he found none. He worried that people would stop coming because there was no space. However, the congregation continued to grow. When they reached fifty, he started a second service. To handle all the people who wanted to study the Bible, he began to have Bible studies every night of the week. God began working miracles in the congregation. The most impressive of these miracles occurred on a Friday evening when the congregation had planned a neighborhood cookout. No one came until fifteen minutes before the cookout was to conclude. Suddenly, people started coming out of their homes and over to the church's duplex. The climax of the event occurred when two young people started walking up the small hill to the church. Quite spontaneously, the young man dropped to his knees and cried out, "I need to be saved!" The young woman, when she saw him do this, also dropped to the ground begging God for forgiveness.

The church continued to grow in that little place until they were reaching more than one hundred seventy people for weekly Bible study and worship. At that point, the church, called Iglesia Bautista Estrella de Belen, moved to share facilities with an aging Anglo congregation located down the street.

About twenty miles to the east was a community that had more churches per square mile than any other place in the region. It also had a high percentage of the population that remained unchurched. Many of these people were a part of the country-western lifestyle characterized by hard-living days and honky-tonk nights. A church, called the Country Church, was started for them. The worship services resembled a dinner theater as much as they did a worship service. The sanctuary contained tables and chairs instead of pews. A country-western band, that really knew how to turn two-step into a hymn, replaced the traditional choir! The messages, all biblical, related to the congregation's lifestyles. Addiction recovery and emotional stability were entry-level discipleship programs. The church did not grow large, but it reached the unchurched in that area with amazing effectiveness.

Cliff Temple Baptist Church, located in the Oak Cliff section of Dallas, Texas, started all three of these churches. Cliff Temple is one of more than three hundred churches that has adopted the One Church, Many Congregations strategy called the Key Church Strategy. The examples described above are just 3 of 28 congregations the church has started since 1992. Other churches have stories that are just as remarkable. The pages of this book contain many of those stories.

The writing of the book has been deliberately delayed for twenty years. The Key Church Strategy began in 1979. Key Church leaders have asked at each training conference, "When are you going to put this material in print?" The authors postponed writing about it until the Key Church Strategy had become a successful and established church planting strategy. It is now time for this publication. As of 1997, which is the last year for which we have statistics, 300 Southern Baptist churches located in 27 different states have adopted the Key Church Strategy. The total Bible study attendance of these churches is 172,152 people!

The authors have worked with Key Churches throughout the United States, and have made "how to" training available to each of the Key Churches. We conducted surveys on a regular basis to measure the effectiveness of the evangelism, ministry, and church starting programs in each of these churches. The responses have been positive.

The purpose for writing this book is to provide a basic guide for churches to develop their own Key Church Strategy. The subject matter presented is in an overview format. We have not tried to present an exhaustive study of missions, but we have attempted to provide enough information for the reader to head in the right direction. With this book a pastor can lead his or her church in the discovery of new ways of influencing the community and advancing the Kingdom of God.

Each chapter is an individual unit of study standing apart from the others. Church leaders can use the material to train different members of the Key Church Council at different times, according to their specific needs and interests. Leaders in church starting, community ministries, and evangelism can quickly discover the section or chapter that pertains to a particular work. We recommend the use of discussion groups to teach the book. The dynamics of group discussions will facilitate the discovery of new and unique ideas for community outreach, especially when members of the discussion group are mature church members who have been interested in missions over an extended period.

1.

FOUNDATIONS

Introduction

The year was 1977. The disciples of Gambrell Street Baptist Church of Fort Worth, Texas, faced a huge challenge. The church's community had changed significantly over the last twenty years, becoming increasingly populated by blue-collar Anglos and Hispanics. Under the dynamic preaching ministry of Dr. Joel Gregory, the church was adding new members rapidly. On the surface, it appeared that this great church was thriving.

A closer examination of the growth told a different story. Most who joined Gambrell Street Church in those days were ministerial students (18 percent), professionals (59 percent), and retirees (19 percent). The vast majority of new members (83 percent) came to the church by transfer from another church. Conversion growth was limited largely to the children of members. The worship services and Bible studies reflected the deep intellectual and classical orientation of the congregation. Not surprisingly, few people from the immediate neighborhood joined the church. Those who did join stayed only for a short period and rarely assimilated into the church.

Troubled by this reality, the mission-minded church sought the mind of God. The question these modern disciples asked God was, "What can we do to build your church among all the diverse groups of people in this community? How shall we bring the good news to our neighbors? They will not come to our services. They will not join our church."

At about the same time, J V Thomas, Director of Project Development for the Baptist General Convention of Texas, conceived of a way for churches like Gambrell Street Church to reach out to the various ethnic groups and subcultures living in their communities. He suggested that the congregation at Gambrell Street Baptist Church become an anchor, or *key* church in the community, through which multiple new congregations would be started. The plan called for these new congregations to reflect the multiple cultures making up their neighborhood.[1]

The One Church, Many Congregations model became a reality with the Gambrell Street project. By 1992, the church consisted of a total of thirty-six congregations in addition to the main campus. Under the leadership of the minister of missions Tim Ahlen,[2] their off-campus ministries included three types of congregations.

1. *Church-type congregations.* These congregations were traditional churches started to reach specific unchurched groups of people. Gambrell Street sponsored ten church-type congregations. They included a Nigerian, two African American, a middle-class Anglo, two Hispanic, a Japanese, a Chinese, a Cambodian and a working-class Anglo church. In each case, the goal was to plant new churches that would one day be completely self-supporting, self-governing, and self-propagating.
2. *Indigenous Satellite Congregations.*[3] These congregations, mostly house churches, ministered to the needs of the blue-collar residents of the surrounding neighborhoods. While each was encouraged to become as autonomous as possible, all parties involved recognized the value of a strong ongoing relationship to the sponsor church. Gambrell Street sponsored nineteen indigenous satellite congregations.
3. *Multihousing congregations.* Seven congregations held services in donated apartments. Multihousing congregations are special examples of indigenous satellite congregations. Like house churches, they also minister to blue-collar people. In

addition to depending on the sponsor church for support, multihousing congregations rely on the apartment management for permission to minister on the property.

To say that the strategy was a success is an understatement. By the end of 1991, the mission congregations were averaging more than 600 in attendance, which was more than the main campus had in attendance. Unlike the sponsor church, the mission congregations received almost half of their new members through conversion and baptism.

Typical of the many success stories coming out of the missions program was the Crossroads Baptist Church. In 1989, Ahlen received a call from the owner of an eighty-five-unit apartment community known as Crossroads Apartments. She had heard of the mission program at Gambrell Street and wanted to know if the church could do for her property what it had done for several others.

The apartment community was low income, racially mixed, and the buildings were in need of repair. A walk around the community showed it was a war zone. Graffiti covered the walls, hypodermic syringes and bullet casings were strewn on the ground, bare dirt was exposed where there should have been grass, and playground equipment was broken through misuse and neglect. After some discussions, the owner of the property promised to donate an apartment to be used as a chapel. She gave permission to the people from Gambrell Street Church to develop a church and to conduct ministries on the property. By the end of 1991, a pastor from the community had been enlisted and trained. The congregation averaged about forty in attendance. Their church program included Sunday school and worship, weeknight prayer meetings, Bible studies, and evangelistic visitation. On Friday nights, the men of the church conducted evangelistic street ministry; on Saturday, they held a worship service in a local nursing home.

The impact of this small congregation was remarkable. One could now walk across the property on a Sunday morning and, instead of the incessant "boom-boom-boom" of secular rock or rap music, the strains of "Amazing Grace" or some other hymn could be heard coming out of the Crossroads Chapel. Instead of bare dirt, grass and flowerbeds now covered the courtyard. The playground equipment had been repaired or replaced by the congregation. Gunshots and drug deals were almost nonexistent. The presence of Christ had transformed the entire community!

Gambrell Street's experience proved to be so successful that the Key Church Strategy became a major program for the Baptist General Convention of Texas. By 1998, more than 165 Texas Baptist churches had formally adopted the strategy. These churches comprised 2 percent of all Texas Southern Baptist churches. They accounted for 36 percent of all new church starts and a corresponding percentage of baptisms. It has been a common experience for these churches to more than double their attendance within two years after adopting the strategy.

To understand why this strategy has been so successful, we need to compare its foundations to those in the New Testament church.

Biblical Foundations

The drama of the moment was intense. Gathered together with the disciples in Caesarea Philippi, Jesus quizzed his followers about his identity. Jesus first asked about popular opinion concerning his identity. All of the answers were complimentary: "Some say John the Baptist . . . Elijah . . . one of the prophets." Jesus then got specific:

> "Who do you say I am?" [He said.]
> Simon Peter answered, "You are the Christ, the Son of the living God."
> Jesus replied, "Blessed are you, Simon son of Jonah, for this was not revealed to you by man, but by my Father in heaven. And I tell you that you are Peter, and on this rock I will build my church, and the gates of Hades will not overcome it. I will give you the keys of the kingdom of heaven; whatever you bind on earth will be bound in heaven, and whatever you loose on earth will be loosed in heaven." (Matthew 16:15-19)

In the midst of that divine disclosure, Jesus birthed the church. Its establishment, growth, and spiritual strength were Jesus' responsibility. However, Jesus also made it plain that his followers were to be a key element of his strategy: *"I will give you the keys of the kingdom of heaven."* They were the stewards of his authority, and the tools of his craft. It was through his followers that Jesus intended to grow his church.

In his last words to his disciples, Jesus informed them of the extent of his expectations:

> Then Jesus came to them and said, "All authority in heaven and on earth has been given to me. Therefore go and make disciples of all nations, baptizing them in the name of the Father and of the Son and of the Holy Spirit, and teaching them to obey everything I have commanded you. And surely I am with you always, to the very end of the age." (Matthew 28:18-20)

The church was to be built by disciples. In the course of their earthly pilgrimage, they were to reach out to all ethnic groups, cultures, and subcultures. They were to evangelize and disciple them so that they, in turn, would evangelize and disciple others. According to Luke, Jesus told them they were not to go out in their own power to win the world. Rather, they were to wait in Jerusalem until the Holy Spirit came upon them, and then they would "be [his] witnesses . . . to the ends of the earth" (Acts 1:8).

By Christ's own command, the church at Jerusalem was to be the hub of a worldwide evangelism and church planting movement—one church with many congregations. One church starting many congregations!

This way of "doing church" is the pattern followed by the first church in Jerusalem. After Pentecost, the Holy Spirit empowered the apostles to preach with boldness, and thousands of people were converted. The large number of baptized believers mentioned in the book of Acts had very few public venues in which to meet. That they met in their homes suggests that there were hundreds of small congregations meeting in and around Jerusalem during this time. The following is an interpretive discussion based on the author's understanding of Luke's narrative in the book of Acts.

The Extension of the Jerusalem Church

Expansion Prepares the Way for Extension

Following Pentecost, the church at Jerusalem enjoyed a remarkable period of expansion, growth, and organization as "the Lord added to their number daily those who were being saved."

In the beginning, the early believers were clearly a fellowship or sect within the larger Jewish tradition and not a separate religious movement.[4] In Acts 3:1, we observe Peter and John going up to the Temple for afternoon prayer. After healing the crippled man at the Gate Beautiful, the two were brought before the Sanhedrin to answer for their conduct.

As time went on, events took place that suggested development of a separate identity for the church. The believers who owned property sold it in order that the poorest of the saints could receive the necessities of life. When Ananias and Sapphira lied about the proceeds of the sale of their property, the apostles, not the Sanhedrin, judged them. People continued to be converted, but now refrained from joining the believers. We can presume their reticence was caused by fear of retribution from the Jewish authorities. After increasing conflict, the Sanhedrin finally arrested John and Peter. They were put in jail for preaching under the authority of Christ.

Ongoing conflicts with Jewish authorities, combined with the need for the Church's organization, finally solidified the separation between Christianity and Judaism. There were now at least two ethnic and socioeconomic groups in the church: the Aramaic-speaking Christians and the Greek-speaking Christians. While they shared the same faith in Christ and, to an extent, the same Jewish background, there was enough cultural and linguistic discontinuity between the groups that they found it difficult to live and worship in harmony.[5]

This discontinuity is evidenced by the controversy between the Greek and Hebrew believers over the treatment of their widows. The apostles clearly recognized the need for leaders indigenous to the Hellenistic culture. They appointed seven spiritual men to care for the widows. Significantly, they were all Hellenistic Jewish Christians—not a Hebrew among them. They became the first appointed leaders apart from the apostolic circle.[6]

The eventual outcome of this controversy was two Christian communities in Jerusalem—one Hellenistic and the other Aramaic. Most scholars agree that these groups remained in close fellowship, but they probably worshiped separately in their own languages. The Seven led the Hellenistic church but still were under the authority of the Twelve.[7]

In spite of the controversy, the church in Jerusalem continued to expand and mature.[8] There are several references in the Acts of the Apostles, chapters 4 through 6, which speak of the numerical growth of the church (Acts 2:41, 47; 4:4; 6:1). The increasing maturity of the churches is seen in their ability to work through conflict and by the koinonia that developed.

Dispersion Throughout Judea and Samaria (Acts 8–11)

Concurrent with the rise of the Hellenistic church in Jerusalem was the general Jewish persecution of Christians. This oppression broke out in earnest with the stoning of Stephen, one of the Seven. Arguably, the most important result of the persecution was that many Christians of Jerusalem were dispersed throughout Judea and Samaria.[9] As these refugees fled to safer cities, they told the remarkable story of the Savior who died and rose again in order to provide for fellowship with God through forgiveness of sin.

A look at the evangelistic ministry of Philip illustrates just how enthusiastically the gospel was received in the areas outside Jerusalem. Still closely connected with the Jerusalem church, Philip went down to Samaria and preached to great crowds, healing many of their sick. Many "believed Philip as he preached the good news of the kingdom of God and the name of Jesus Christ, they were baptized, both men and women" (Acts 8:12). When the apostles in Jerusalem heard that the Samaritans were being converted to Christianity, they sent Peter and John to oversee the situation. The two apostles confirmed Philip's work and prayed that the new believers might receive the Holy Spirit. The apostles laid their hands upon the new believers, who at that time received the Holy Spirit. This event is notable because it shows not only the establishment of new communities of believers but also the continuing direct involvement of the mother church in Jerusalem. At the leading of the Holy Spirit, Philip headed down the southern road from Jerusalem toward Gaza. Along the way, he encountered an Ethiopian, a eunuch of the court of Candace, whom he won to Christ and baptized. Next, Philip traveled to Azotus and on to Caesarea where he finally settled and raised a family of four daughters, all of whom became preachers.

Following the account of the conversion of Saul in chapter 9 and Peter's ministry to Cornelius in chapter 10, the narrative picks up with the establishment of the church in Antioch. Some unnamed disciples, forced to leave Jerusalem because of the persecution, began preaching in Antioch. Apparently of Hebrew origin, they took it upon themselves to preach only to Jews. At the same time, some men from Cyprus and Cyrene preached to the Gentiles. This preaching resulted in the winning of many converts and the planting of new churches.

When the church at Jerusalem heard what was happening, they sent Barnabas to Antioch to investigate. When he arrived, being impressed by what God was doing, Barnabas went to Tarsus to enlist Paul's help to establish the church. The two stayed in Antioch for a year instructing the people. At the conclusion of the year, the congregation voluntarily took up an offering for the church in Jerusalem—an indication of respect, fellowship, and concern for the church that had been responsible for their own birth.

The Extension of the Antioch Church

When Paul and Barnabas returned after delivering the Antioch donation to the Jerusalem saints, they found the church at Antioch mature enough to begin planting churches of its own. The pattern of One Church, Many Congregations was again established as the church at Antioch set apart Paul and Barnabas for the task of beginning new churches.

The First Missionary Journey

During that first missionary journey, the two church planters began in Cyprus where there had already been some evangelistic work. From there they went to Pisidian Antioch, Iconium, and Lystra, before returning to Antioch. In each place, Paul and Barnabas planted churches following the same pattern of evangelism. They first entered the local synagogue and preached to the Jews. After some initial success, the Jews would turn against them, at which point the missionaries turned their attention to the non-Jews of the city. Overall, this method proved very successful.

When Paul and Barnabas returned to Antioch, they gathered the church together for the purpose of reporting their results to the church. The report was likely well received, given the significant number of Gentiles connected to the church at Antioch. It may have been here that some questions arose concerning the gospel and its spread to the Gentiles. It became necessary to make a trip to Jerusalem for a conference with the leaders of the church at Jerusalem.

The key issue needing to be settled was whether Gentile believers were obligated to observe the Jewish Law, especially at the point of circumcision, in order to become Christians. Paul and Barnabas set before the apostles and elders the gospel they were preaching. They also reported everything God was doing through them—how the Gentiles were coming to Christ and how God was doing miracles in their lives.

In response, one of the believers who belonged to the party of the Pharisees stood up and insisted that the Gentile believers must also be circumcised and obey the Law. Appealing to his own experience, Peter argued against this, saying that God had bestowed the same Holy Spirit on Gentile converts that he had on Jewish converts. He stated forcefully that all people were saved by the grace of God and not by observing the Law.

After everyone had a chance to speak, James, the leader of the Jerusalem church, spoke up and recommended that the only requirements of the Law Gentiles needed to follow was that they not eat meat sacrificed to idols. Additionally, they were to abstain from sexual immorality and not eat the meat of strangled animals.

The letter sent to the Antioch church conveying the sentiments of the Council is significant because of the light it sheds on the authority of the Jerusalem church. It notes that certain members of the Jerusalem church "went out from us without our authorization and disturbed you, troubling your minds by what they said" (Acts 15:24). In other words, people who did not have the approval of the Jerusalem church had no authority in the churches.

Following the decision of the Council, they sent Judas Barsabbas and Silas back to Antioch to represent the Jerusalem church. The two men delivered the opinion of the apostles to the church at Antioch, which they gladly received as encouraging news. The response of the Christians at Antioch shows that, while they may have been functioning autonomously, the relationship between Jerusalem and Antioch was strong. The Jerusalem opinion was very important.

The Second Missionary Journey

The second missionary journey had a different purpose from the first one. The first missionary journey was undertaken to begin new churches. The second journey's stated purpose was to revisit those towns in which they had established churches to see how they were doing and to strengthen them. Paul revisited Derbe, Lystra, Iconium, and Pisidian Antioch. In each town, he delivered the decision of the apostles and elders of Jerusalem, strengthening the churches in their faith.

There was one major difference between the first and second missionary journey. Paul had a significant disagreement with Barnabas over John Mark's suitability for ministry. He separated from Barnabas and took along Silas instead. Although there was a seeming lack of unity between Paul and Barnabas, both men received the blessing of the Antioch church as they left.

Continuing westward from Pisidian Antioch, Paul and Silas came to Troas and continued on to Philippi where they worked for an extended period of time. A consequence of their stay was the establishment of a church in the home of Lydia and the baptism of the Philippian jailer and his family.

Other stops along the way included Thessalonica, Berea, Athens, and Corinth. In each place, they followed the same pattern; Paul and Silas began to preach in the synagogues. After some early success, the Jewish establishment rose in opposition to Paul's message and tried with varying success to run him out of town. Paul then turned his attention to establishing a church among the Gentiles.

Paul and Silas left Corinth after a year and a half, stopping off at Ephesus for a short time before returning to their home church in Antioch.

The Third Missionary Journey

Paul stayed in Antioch for an undetermined amount of time. When he left, he went back through Tarsus into the areas of Phrygia and Galatia to strengthen the existing churches. He returned to Ephesus, where he stayed for three years and established a strong church. Paul then moved on to Macedonia. He spent three months in ministry to Troas, Miletus, Tyre, and Caesarea. Unlike the other missionary journeys, Paul concluded this one by traveling to Jerusalem, where he prepared for his trip to Rome.

The church that began in Jerusalem in the early thirties began as one congregation made up of a few disciples. It grew quickly after Pentecost, as the Holy Spirit empowered the apostles to preach with such boldness that thousands of people were converted. As the church continued to grow, and the ethnic and language distinction became a factor, new congregations were born out of it. The dispersion caused by the Jewish persecution became a pivotal event in the life of the church. All over the Roman Empire, believers began to share their faith with the pagan world around them.

Throughout these early years, there continued to be a tremendous amount of loyalty and respect for the church in Jerusalem and the teaching of the Apostles. Because of the strong relationships, the Jerusalem church was granted authority over the new congregations as they came into being. The authority, while strongly administered under the guidance of the Holy Spirit, was not of the controlling kind. Rather, it was used to build up, encourage, and guide the new congregations to maturity.

This biblical strategy is identical to what the authors call the Key Church Strategy. In the context of the twentieth-century Christian church, a Key Church is one that elevates its local mission strategy to the same level as its education, music, and evangelistic ministries.

Indigenous Foundations

The secret to successful implementation of the Key Church Strategy is to have a working understanding of the indigenous principle. Application of the indigenous principle will enhance the effectiveness of evangelism, discipleship development, and church starting. *The indigenous missions principle states that congregations are healthier and more productive, and require little or no outside support, when started and developed in the context of the socioeconomic conditions and culture of the people who are to be evangelized or congregationalized.* It is logical to believe that using the indigenous mission principle leads to indigenous churches. Melvin L. Hodges, one of the early communicators of the indigenous church planting principle, argues that the New Testament church was indigenous. By indigenous, Hodges meant the following:

1) *Indigenous churches were self-propagating.* In other words, they raised up their own workers and spread the gospel by their own means.
2) *Indigenous churches were self-governing.* That is, they were governed by members who came from the target community.
3) *Indigenous churches were self-supporting.* They were not dependent on outside funds to meet the ministry needs of the church.

"The New Testament Churches were not dependent on workers or funds from a foreign field but were self-sufficient as local units."[10]

There is more to the indigenous principle and indigenous churches than these three "self's". William A. Smalley, in his article entitled "Cultural Implications of an Indigenous Church," states that culture is a very important consideration for indigenous church planting. He defines an indigenous church as: "a group of believers who live out their life, including their socialized Christian activity, in the patterns of the local society, and for whom any transformation of that society comes out of their felt needs under the guidance of the Holy Spirit and the Scriptures."[11]

Culture forms the matrix in which people's lives are shaped. Things like values, codes of conduct, dress, language, family, attitudes, and many other human characteristics are imparted by culture. People are influenced by the culture in which they are born, grow up, live, work, and play. The further a person is removed from his or her culture the more difficulty he or she experiences in coping, adapting, and feeling comfortable. The greater the change, the greater the stress, and the more difficult it is to become acclimated to the new culture.

Place this discussion in the context of the mission of the church, and one begins to see the tension between a church established in one culture and an unchurched people living in a different culture. In order to minister effectively, the cultural barriers must be lowered. The gospel message and the expressions of worship, discipleship, outreach, and organization must be contextualized to the target culture. For example, consider the following two churches in the 1980s. Greenlaw Baptist Church was a blue-collar church located in Flagstaff, in the mountains of northern Arizona. Its people valued practical, "hands-on" expression of Christianity. They came to church in informal dress. They were highly evangelistic. They enjoyed shouting "Amen" when the preacher delivered the main points of his sermon. It was an unusual Sunday that the altar was not filled with people recommitting their lives to Christ during the invitation. The music was lively, consisting mostly of Stamps Baxter–style gospel songs, and accompanied by guitar and piano. People regularly and freely expressed their emotions. Compare Greenlaw Church's culture to the Ridgecrest Baptist Church of New Windsor, New York. This church was very close to the West Point Military Academy. Many of its members were captains and majors in the army. Unlike Greenlaw Church, these Christians felt the best way of worshiping God was to sit at attention in silence for an hour. They wore suits and dresses to church. The songs that they enjoyed singing were the great old hymns of the faith, accompanied by a classical piano or organ. It was unheard of for someone to show emotions or go to the altar for prayer.

Both congregations saw their way of doing church as *the* biblical way and would not have felt comfortable in the other congregation. Ridgecrest members would have considered Greenlaw Church to be lacking in dignity and reverence. Greenlaw's members would have considered Ridgecrest Church to be spiritually dead and cold. In fact, both churches were faithful to the Scriptures in the way they did church. Both churches were indigenous to their cultures. Had either of these two churches tried planting *their* kind of church in the other's community, they would have failed. However, since indigenous principles were used to plant them, both churches thrived.

The lesson to be learned here is this: To apply the indigenous principle, mission leaders must base their strategy, methods, and ministries on Scripture, and not on their own cultural interpretation of the Bible. The principles of Scripture must then be applied in the context of the target, rather than the host, culture.

How does a single congregation church become multicultural, multicongregational, and focus the gospel message to all kinds of people? The Key Church Strategy is the answer. The following thirteen principles will help interpret this chapter on the indigenous principle.

1. Take the gospel to people of different cultures. Do not passively wait for them to come to you. Contemporary American churches are overly optimistic about the appeal of their church programs to people of different cultures. On the contrary, American church culture can be very intimidating to those who are not inside it. Although people of different cultures may be interested in Christ, they will find him best in the context of their own culture.

2. Allow the resulting church to develop within the indigenous culture. Avoid the tendency to export the sponsor church's own culture to the target community. Again, American ethnocentricity can be a very negative factor when it comes to reaching new ethnic and cultural groups.

3. Recognize that socioeconomic and lifestyle factors affect culture as much as language and the country of birth. For example, the difference between blue-collar northern Arizona and New Windsor, New York cultures is immense.

4. Expect the new congregation to express itself differently from yours. (Your church has its own culture.) One of the saddest conversations I have ever had with a missionary was one I had with a retiree who had ministered in pre-Castro Cuba. In the late 1980s this dear, but misguided, soul had an opportunity to go back to Cuba for a visit. Upon her return she told me that she praised the Lord. After all these years, the Cuban churches had *finally learned to play Mendelssohn in their churches!* They no longer sang all those silly *corritos!*

5. Send out leaders from the sponsoring church into the culturally different community. However, keep the total number of such leaders to a minimum. Too many will intimidate the people you are trying to reach.

6. Employ missionary methods. Teach members of the church planting team to replace themselves by enlisting residents indigenous to the target community and teaching them to be leaders. The church planting team is to return to the sponsoring church within a year or take another assignment in a different congregation.

7. Let the people's perceived needs determine the strategy, programs, and ministries. You may be right in your assessment of what the target population's ultimate need is. However, if they do not see it that way, you will lose the opportunity to influence their lives for Christ. The wise missionary will start by applying the gospel to whatever needs the people perceive as being most important. Over time, under the guidance of the Holy Spirit, they will come to understand more about their ultimate needs.

8. Discover, and then plug into, the community's existing assets and resources. Avoid making the arrogant assumption that the people you are trying to reach lack the capability, discernment, financial resources, and leaders to minister to one another or to start a church. The people of that community invariably have a better grasp of community problems than the church planting team. And, they are usually quite capable of solving them.

9. Serve for the Kingdom's sake—not your own and not your church's! This is, after all, God's business. We are his servants.

10. Expect problems. If something can go wrong, it probably will. Most problems can be avoided by being proactive and communicating clearly with the mission congregation. The unavoidable ones can usually be solved with a little ingenuity and guidance from the Holy Spirit.

11. Expect great blessings from God because you are obedient to the Great Commission.

12. Expect to experience accelerated church growth. Churches typically double their total church attendance (including mission congregations) within about two years.

13. Keep financial support at a minimum. Avoid spending large amounts of money subsidizing pastors' salaries or mission church budgets. Use volunteers whenever possible. Start with a low-budget approach, and allow the finances to come from the new people being reached.

Practical Foundations

To implement the indigenous principle requires a person or a group of people to cross the cultural, language, and other barriers separating them from the target culture. As they cross these barriers, church planters cannot strip themselves entirely of their own culture. Because of this fact, *there is no such thing as a completely indigenous new church at the outset of any missionary enterprise.* Indigenization is a process, the goal of which is to produce a church that reflects the cultural and social patterns of the target population.

At this point, a variety of practical issues rises to the surface. How does one apply the indigenous principle and still deal with the practical side of missions? How can a church be a good sponsor? What kind of strategic planning can a sponsor do with an indigenous congregation? How does an indigenous congregation secure a pastor? How do sponsors help an indigenous congregation financially? How do they help indigenous congregations with buildings? What about debt, real estate purchases, and building design? How do sponsors communicate with indigenous congregations? How do they solve problems within the fellowship of indigenous congregations? These questions address the basic issues in the daily operations of mission work.

The remainder of this chapter is dedicated to answering these questions. The following discussion illustrates the need for persons who make missionary decisions to be sensitive to the indigenous mission principle.

Sponsorship

Using the Key Church Strategy, established churches plant and support new congregations, in effect sponsoring them until they are capable of supporting and maintaining their own ministry. In some cases, sponsorship becomes a colonial enterprise through which a "parent" church births a "daughter" church that grows up to look just like the parent. Until the daughter church can be trusted to behave like the parent, the parent maintains tight control over the church's finances and activities. Colonial church planting strategies have unfortunately been employed too frequently in the history of the church. The resulting churches are usually sterile and out of touch with the people they are trying to reach.

In the Key Church context, sponsorship is a *partnership* between the new church congregation and the established church. Each partner supplies some expertise and resources needed to begin and grow a new church. The sponsor church provides a strong doctrinal foundation, mature Christian leadership, and financial resources. The new congregation, even when it is very small, provides an understanding of the targeted community's culture and the local relationships important for church growth. The goal of sponsorship is for the sponsoring church's presence to decrease as the new congregation grows. The sponsor can call itself successful if it works itself out of a job.

Understanding Culture

Before starting, the sponsor church must have a basic understanding of the culture of the specific group of people targeted for the new church or ministry. If the targeted culture is the same as that of the sponsoring church, the sponsor can take considerable initiative in the church planting process. If the culture is distinctly different from the sponsor's, the sponsor church will be more successful if it takes the time to find leaders from the targeted community who speak the language and understand the culture. In this case, assistance from the sponsoring church should be short-term and project-oriented. Rather than conducting the ministries of the new church themselves, volunteers should train indigenous leaders to do the ministry.

The importance of these principles can be illustrated by the experience of Cliff Temple Baptist Church in the starting of Iglesia Bautista Estrella de Belen. In 1992, Cliff Temple sent four well-trained individuals into a predominantly Hispanic neighborhood to start a new church. Each member of the church planting team was fluent in Spanish and had some understanding of the target community's culture. The only negative working against them was that they were all Anglo.

The team worked hard to establish relationships in the community for a solid year. The community was friendly and came to trust the church people enough to allow their children to attend Bible clubs and other activities. However, the adults just would not participate in any of the activities.

Finally, Ben Lopez, a Hispanic layman from the community, became interested in the new work and agreed to become its pastor. Within a matter of three months, the congregation was averaging about forty in attendance. About half of the congregation was made up of adults. Over the next two years the congregation showed solid growth and became a church through which God was very active.

Planning

Sponsor and new church leaders who share the same culture can sit down together, plan together, and make consensual decisions. Sponsor and new church leaders from different cultures find planning to be much more difficult.

In a cross-cultural situation, it is best for the sponsor to work with the new church pastor and lay leaders, letting them take the initiative. Ask the new church leaders what they will lead the congregation to do, how they plan to do it, and how much will it cost. The use of open-ended questions is one way sponsoring church leaders can determine needs, plans, and direction from the new church's leadership. An old adage that has guided planning with new church congregations is, "No one is lazy except in the pursuit of someone else's idea." Some initiative needs to be taken by the sponsor church in order to make progress, but too much initiative from persons outside the congregation takes away ownership. When ownership is taken away, local initiative stops.

Pastor Selection

The most important ingredient in starting new churches is pastoral leadership. The right pastor in the right place will nearly always produce good results. The wrong pastor in the wrong place can be disastrous. How can sponsoring churches determine God's will in finding the right pastor?

The first place to start is prayer. "When he saw the crowds, he had compassion on them, because they were harassed and helpless, like sheep without a shepherd. Then he said to his disciples, 'The harvest is plentiful but the workers are few. Ask [pray] the Lord of the harvest, therefore, to send out workers into his harvest field'" (Matthew 9:36-38). Prayer is the most important tool in leadership selection. God's guidance eliminates mistakes.

Profile the new church that is to be started. Look at qualities such as language, culture, education, income, and lifestyle of the people targeted for the new church. What is the potential for growth? If this new venture succeeds, what kind of pastor will the church need five years from the starting point?

Profile the prospective founding pastor. Instruct new church leaders to determine the kind of pastor they would look for if they were on a pastor search committee five years in the future. Issues to consider are (1) spiritual maturity, (2) cultural/ethnic background, (3) education/training, (4) socioeconomic background,

(5) leadership style, (6) reputation in the community, and (7) denominational background. The ideal pastor will fit the resulting profile. The further away congregations move from this ideal, the further away they move from the indigenous principle.

Enlist the help of your denomination's local or regional judicatories to find a pastor who matches the profile. In most instances there will be qualified individuals available. In those cases where an indigenous pastor cannot be found through the usual denominational channels, look to the target community itself. Enlist one or more of the community's Christian leaders to serve as the leader of the church. It may be a little tricky to find a way to fit this person into the denomination's hierarchy—it may not be possible to call the person "pastor." However, the benefits of using an indigenous person to lead the congregation far outweigh the organizational challenges.

Funding

Funding is the area where the indigenous principle is most often ignored. Seldom are denominational funding resources made available to sponsoring churches in the context of good indigenous missions. It is easy for sponsoring churches to equate church starting with benevolence. The most common philosophy on funding is "the poorer the people, the greater the amount of financial resources going into the ministry." This may seem logical on the surface, but in reality the opposite is true. When ministering to persons who are economically disadvantaged, it is very easy to help too much. **A good rule-of-thumb is to never fund 100 percent; never do anything for a new church congregation that they can do for themselves. A corollary to this rule is to never do for a group of people anything they could not ultimately do for themselves.**

Funding for economically disadvantaged congregations can best be accomplished through fund-raising projects. Matching gifts on a dollar per dollar (or other) ratio is a great way to help without taking church ownership from the congregation. Long-term, monthly supplements of pastors' salaries or church budgets communicate a welfare mentality, and it takes the sense of ownership, responsibility, and incentive from the congregation. It also has the potential to make the pastor, rather than the congregation, responsible to funding agencies.

Funding economically healthy congregations can be accomplished through matching gifts, by supporting the budget, or subsidizing rent or mortgage payments for church facilities. Planning for funding can be successfully negotiated face-to-face when working in the context of middle-class new churches working with middle-class sponsoring/partnering churches.

Facilities

The development of appropriate church facilities is another area where indigenous principles are crucial to long-term health of a new congregation. Unfortunately, many sponsoring churches operate on the belief that everybody's church ought to look just like theirs. Consequently, new congregations find that they are overloading themselves with debt, dreaming about a facility they could never afford on their own, or meeting in a place that is not compatible with their culture. The following is a good illustration of the importance of using indigenous principles to develop church facilities.

The North American Mission Board (SBC), in an attempt to practice better indigenous missions, began to transfer ownership of mission buildings to the congregations meeting in the buildings. A Native American congregation was presented the deed to the building where they had been meeting for many years. The building was heated with a propane central unit. Sponsors had paid for the propane gas for many years. But the congregation understood the building was now theirs. They were responsible for maintaining it and paying all the utility bills. Later, a missionary visiting the congregation was surprised to find a wood stove being used instead of the central unit. He asked the pastor what had happened to the central heating unit. "Was it broken?"

"No," the pastor replied.

There was a simple explanation. While the Native Americans could cut the wood, they could not afford to purchase propane. If only the Mission Board had thought, they could have saved several years of expense on heating bills. One wonders if the Native American congregation would have put wood stoves in the building when it was constructed if it had been their building and their responsibility to pay for fuel. Probably so.

The moral of this story is that buildings should be purchased in the context of the congregation's ability to pay and in the context of their culture. Do not do for them what they can do for themselves, and conversely, do not do for them what they could not ultimately do for themselves.

Many times through the purchase of facilities, financial support, and phaseout of financial assistance, goals are set by the helping agencies that are impossible for the new church to meet. Unrealistic goals, and goals set by others, set new churches up for failure. When a church fails, lives are adversely affected. This is the opposite of good indigenous missions. It is the opposite of Christian love and compassion. I have never known a new church that could not find a place to meet. The life or death of a new church does not depend on a building. However, backbreaking debt and lack of ownership can become life or death issues for new church congregations.

Communication

Communication is a two-way street! It is like the yo-yo on the string. In order for the yo-yo to work, the string has to unwind and then rewind. Good communication is the key to good relationships between sponsoring churches and the new congregations they develop. Poor communications result in misunderstanding, burned bridges, and, sometimes, antagonism resulting in a permanent dissolution of relationship between the two churches. Most often, the main problem in communications is that the messages only go in one direction. The sponsor church "tells" the new congregation what to do. Instead of dialoguing with the new church, the sponsor monologues. It never stops to listen, never stops to check if the message, so eloquently delivered, was ever actually understood. **One-way communication is not only bad indigenous missions, but bad manners as well.**

Communication is made more difficult when crossing language and cultural barriers. Cross-cultural understanding is very important to good communication. For example, in a face-saving culture, you will discover that *yes* does not always mean *yes.* Sometimes it means "I respect you too much to embarrass you by saying *no* to your face." In another culture where relationships are more important than productivity, "Yankee ingenuity" might be more insulting than helpful, especially when it undercuts the pastor of the new congregation.

The church that plans to plant new churches within different cultures should take advantage of every opportunity to learn something about those cultures. Get some materials on cross-cultural communication from local bookstores or appropriate denominational judicatories.

Regular meetings with each new congregation pastor will greatly enhance communications. Soon after becoming minister of missions of one of our new Key Churches, the author set up a breakfast meeting with all the new church pastors. The Cambodian pastor came to the meeting with his daughter, who served as his interpreter. We ate together, enjoyed good fellowship, and prayed together. The Cambodian pastor began to weep. Then he expressed his gratitude for being invited to the breakfast. He stated that this was the first invitation in seven years for fellowship with other Christian leaders in the church. This good church did not intend to leave this wonderful pastor out of their fellowship. They just never planned to include him because he did not speak their language. Love-in-action is the best communication tool for leaders interested in indigenous mission.

Problem Solving

Problems are a part of the "package" if churches become involved in new church starting. Sponsorship problems, leadership problems, theological problems, financial problems, and miscommunication problems face mission leaders every day.

Problems viewed from the point of confident faith are opportunities. Problems that are being solved bring people together. It is during difficult times that people grow in Christ and deepen their relationships with one another. It is very easy to step over the line of good indigenous missions when dealing with problems. Ownership can be taken away from a new church very easily during times of crisis. Special care needs to be taken in relation to initiative during these times. Work with the leaders involved to define the problem. Do this without assessing blame. Remove as much tension and emotion as possible. Help the new church leaders list options. Pray for the right spirit. Pray for God's help to do the right thing. Work with the new church leadership to find a consensus if possible. It is best to discuss problems in a one-on-one relationship or in small groups. Many times, new churches live or die because of the way problems are handled. It is possible for the process of seeking a solution to cause more damage than the problem itself. Problems cannot be solved in a positive manner unless there are positive relationships with leaders in the sponsoring church and the new church congregation.

In one low-income, multifamily housing church, we had worked hard to develop, train, and put in place indigenous leaders. We finally succeeded in enlisting a man who served as an "associate" in another local church to become the pastor. The man earned his living as a baker. He had an eighth-grade education, but was spiritually mature and very knowledgeable in the Bible. His wife was an enthusiastic partner to her husband, and assumed many of the teaching responsibilities.

About three months after bringing him on board, we received a complaint from one of the members that the pastor's wife was using Bible study material published by a nationally renowned preacher of the so-called prosperity gospel. We gently asked the pastor's wife about her Bible study material. Her response was interesting. She said, "Oh, yes, I use Brother ———'s material. He really speaks to the needs of our people!" When we probed a little further, it became obvious—the people in this community were poor, unhealthy, and failures at almost everything they had tried in life. What they yearned for was for God to tell them how to be healthy, wealthy, and prosperous.

Our first response was to go down to the local Baptist bookstore to find some Bible study material that would fit the needs of the people in the apartment community. Imagine our surprise (if you are not a Baptist, *you* may not be surprised but *we* were!) when we found out that none of the Baptist publishing houses had Bible study material that showed poor, unhealthy people how to be healthy, wealthy, and prosperous!

We now had a dilemma. How were we to preserve the dignity, leadership, and autonomy of this local congregation and at the same time keep the church within the bounds of acceptable doctrine? What we finally did was set up a task force made up of members from both congregations, and we developed our own curriculum based on our common reading of the pertinent biblical texts. The mission congregation felt comfortable with the material, and the sponsoring congregation felt relieved that the problem had been solved.

Epilogue

In 1992, the Gambrell Street Baptist Church reevaluated its church planting ministry and concluded that it would be better for the church if they scaled back their missions ministry. The feeling was that if they concentrated their efforts on building up the home base, the church would grow. In fact, quite the opposite occurred. The main campus now averages a little under three hundred in attendance, down from more than one thousand at its peak. The church still sponsors only eight mission churches. They average about one hundred and fifty in attendance, down from more than six hundred at its peak. Their overall community impact has decreased by about 70 percent.

Even though it does much less local mission work than it used to, Gambrell Street Baptist Church still does more than other churches of its size, and it continues to excel by participating in foreign missions work.

2.

HOW DOES IT WORK?

Introduction

In the 1950s, the Oak Cliff section of Dallas, Texas, was typical of American suburbia. Primarily a home for middle- to upper-income Anglo-Americans, people considered Oak Cliff *the* place to live in Dallas. As was common in suburban communities like this, Oak Cliff boasted a large number of churches. One of them was Cliff Temple Baptist Church. Begun in 1908 as a mission of another church, Cliff Temple was in every sense of the word a neighborhood church. As the Oak Cliff community grew, so did Cliff Temple. Soon it was one of the largest Baptist churches in Dallas, second only to First Baptist Church.

In the mid-1950s, however, the Oak Cliff community began to change. African Americans and Hispanics began to move into the area. White flight began to take place, and as it did, most of the churches fled as well. Cliff Temple, under the leadership of pastors Wallace Bassett (1918–1966), Doug Waterston, Dan Griffin, and Dean Dickens (1989–1996), decided to stay and minister in the new community.

Because of its large membership and commitment to community ministries, Cliff Temple remained a viable, vibrant church, while most others found it difficult to keep the doors open. By 1990, however, Cliff Temple had become a large and graying church. According to one analysis of the membership rolls conducted at this time, there were 1800 active members in the church, but the *median age was seventy-two!*

The new ethnic groups moving into Oak Cliff began some new churches indigenous to the new cultures, but they could not keep up with the pace of the transition. There was a large spiritual vacuum. Filling that vacuum required the planting of dozens of new churches.

Cliff Temple, under the leadership of Pastor Dean Dickens, decided to adopt the Key Church Strategy. They called J V Thomas to prepare the church by laying the groundwork for the new strategy. He worked there for a year, strategizing, teaching, promoting, and praying with the leaders in the church.

In January 1992, the church called Tim Ahlen to serve as full-time minister of missions in order to integrate their church planting, community ministries, and evangelism programs into one staff position.

The church already had a sizable community ministries program. Their food pantry served emergency food supplies to almost eight thousand people each year. They had a clothing closet, several life skills programs, seasonal events, and numerous other contacts in the community.

Ahlen's job assignment was to maintain the community ministries program and to focus on church planting. In three years, Cliff Temple Baptist Church began more than twenty-five new congregations of various kinds. Some were churches located in apartment communities. Others were niche churches that filled a spiritual vacuum in a particular subculture—for example, the country-western lifestyle. The church also planted new congregations in predominantly Hispanic or African American communities.

Over the three-year period, the total weekly attendance of the mission congregations of the church grew from around one hundred to more than eight hundred. More than half of the growth was from conversions. Partially because of the church planting effort, the opportunities for community ministries increased. In fact, the opportunities for ministry so outstripped the available church resources that MISSION: Oak Cliff, Inc. (a 501(c)(3) non-profit corporation) was established.

How was success of this magnitude possible? Of course, the credit goes to God. Mere human strategies, efforts, and organizations cannot explain this kind of growth. God used several significant factors to extend his kingdom through Cliff Temple. Any church serious about preparing for a powerful work of God should employ these factors.

Lay a Foundation

The first factor making the rapid extension possible was that a firm foundation was laid. Although the need for new churches had existed for many years, Cliff Temple did not implement the Key Church Strategy until the church was prepared.

Cliff Temple's church planting foundation was laid over a period of several decades. Over the years, the church started and supported eight new churches. Most of these churches were started individually. Cliff Temple sometimes found itself working with more than one church at a time. This kind of committed sponsorship gave them valuable experience to oversee a larger scale missions program.

Cliff Temple's involvement in community ministries was an important factor contributing to a firm foundation. Dating back to the late 1940s, the community ministries program not only met the human and spiritual concerns of the needy, but also served to build up a level of trust and confidence in the Oak Cliff community. When the Key Church Strategy began, there was already a community-wide appreciation and support for the work of the church.

Another important factor was the work of J V Thomas during the year before launching the Key Church Strategy. Although Cliff Temple had already been involved in new church sponsorship and community ministries, the leadership of the church still did not understand the strategy. Mr. Thomas spent the better part of the year educating and training the chief leaders of the church about the ministry. When they finally implemented the strategy in 1992, the primary decision makers in the church understood what was taking place.

The Cliff Temple story provides some important principles for any church considering implementing the Key Church Strategy.

To lay a firm foundation for this approach to ministry, a church should consider the following:

1. Is there a need to implement the Key Church Strategy? Many factors can help a church determine the need for new congregations. A survey of population trends will show whether any ethnic, racial, or cultural transitions are taking place in the community. Transitional communities usually provide the most fertile fields for new church starts. New and rapidly growing communities are also indications of a need for new churches. In some communities, existing churches are older and plateaued, indicating the need for new churches as well. If a significant percentage of unchurched people live in the community, several new churches can be started. These churches can operate at a "beginner" level, teaching the new members at their own level of spiritual understanding.

An excellent way to determine the need for the Key Church Strategy is to conduct a community survey as part of a long-range strategic planning process. *The Key Church Long Range Planning Guide*, **by J V Thomas and Tim Ahlen, helps the local church leadership to look at the community with eyes geared for church planting and community ministries. After developing a list of needs, the leadership meets in a retreat setting. The purpose of the retreat is to prioritize those needs, match them with local resources, and set goals and action plans for a three to five year period.**

2. Is the church committed to planting new congregations? Churches and denominations differ as to how they define "missions." Some consider missions to be ministry to the poor. Others consider any kind of outreach to be missions. Still, others consider missions to involve trips to far away places. All of these ministries are valuable forms of Christian work. They all may be part of a Key Church's missions program. The Key Church is unique because it is *always* committed to planting new congregations.

3. Does the church already know how to sponsor a new congregation? The ideal Key Church will have one or more successful church starts under its belt when it begins to implement the strategy. If it has never planted a new church, then it is wise for the church to start one before attempting multiple church starts.

4. Does the church have a strong and positive reputation in the community as a caring church? A good reputation helps build trust with the ethnic and cultural groups being targeted for evangelism. Some churches may not have been involved in the community. Others may have had some negatives in their history with respect to community relationships. In both cases, it is important to build good relationships before embarking on a strategy that the community might view as invasive or colonial.

5. Does the church leadership understand the Key Church Strategy? Most church members love their church so much that they assume that everyone in the world would love it if they could just get them to come. Church leaders typically have the mind-set that the ultimate goal of every church is to grow their congregation as large as possible. A lack of understanding of indigenous church planting and church growth principles can result in the leadership viewing the strategy as one that drains rather than enhances the overall ministry of the church. An informed leadership is essential to the laying of a foundation for the Key Church Strategy. The planning process mentioned above will provide the needed education.

Establish a Vision

Dean Dickens came to Cliff Temple in 1989 after having served sixteen years as a missionary in the Philippines. Cliff Temple called him to be their pastor in part because the church leadership had a hazy vision of their ex-neighborhood church staying in its urban location and reaching the community through a comprehensive missions strategy. Leaders of Cliff Temple did not fully understand the implications of their desires. When Dr. Dickens came on board, he combined his own vision with that of the leadership. He used his missionary background and communication skills to begin articulating the Key Church vision to the congregation in a way that took the "haze" off.

Dr. Dickens' articulation of that vision was a two-edged sword. For some in the congregation, especially the leadership, the newly clarified vision motivated them to begin implementing an effective missioning strategy. For others, the idea of staying in their urban location was really nothing more than wistful nostalgia. As long as the vision was sufficiently unclear, these people could give assent, hoping that the result of a Key Church Strategy would be a return to Cliff Temple's heyday of the 1950s. Eventually, it became clear that a bold missions strategy would bring about fundamental change in the church. They realized that there were giants in the land and they were "sore afraid."

In the end, the majority of the congregation realized that the Key Church vision was a Kingdom vision. They sensed it was what God wanted them to do and so they voted to pursue that vision with all of God's resources available.

It is not *always* necessary to *see* where you are going to *get* where you're going, but it sure helps. To establish a clear Key Church vision for the local church, the pastor must show church members (1) what the final product is expected to look like, (2) what remains to be accomplished before they can claim to have arrived, and (3) how far they have come since they began the journey.

Communicating the Key Church vision to the local church requires a multipronged approach. It involves (1) several strong, biblical sermons highlighting both the Great Commission mandate and the pressing needs in the community; (2) publication of articles in the church newsletter, posters and other forms of publicity explaining various aspects of the strategy; (3) study and discussion groups that explore the issues and work through the questions people have; (4) field trips, where possible, to churches already using the strategy; and (5) church leadership that works with the pastor to spread the vision.

Establish an Organization

In 1992, Cliff Temple had a strong rotating committee structure. As minister of missions, Ahlen had four committees assigned to him: the Missions Committee, the Weekday Ministries Committee, the Women's Missionary Union, and the Evangelism Committee. Each of these committees played a vital role in the missions program. The only problem was that the committees never met together. They never planned together and they lacked the kind of interdependence needed for the smooth operation of a missions program.

Besides the committees having direct involvement in the missions program, there were individuals and groups that needed to support the mission activities. Most of the new mission congregations needed help to establish Sunday schools. Others needed help with construction projects. The deacon body and the finance committee needed to be involved.

One of Ahlen's first jobs was to implement an organizational structure. The goal was to bring all these entities together in a way that facilitated the starting of churches and ministries. The result was establishment of the Key Church Council. This council was made up of the chairpersons of the four groups directly involved in missions. Representatives (not necessarily the chairpersons) from the deacons, the Finance Committee, and the Sunday school served on the council. People were appointed to serve as mission trips director, publicity director, secretary, and chairperson. The Key Church Council met at least monthly in order to plan and coordinate the overall missions ministry of the church.

The Weekday Ministries, Missions, and Evangelism Committees were then organized so that each church planting project, ministry, or event had a project director responsible for it. A necessary part of any church ministry strategy is the establishment of an organizational structure that will do more than simply meet and make decisions. Good organizational structures facilitate ministry, not merely debate it. For an example of how the Key Church Council can be organized, see appendix 1.

Discover Mission Opportunities

Mission opportunities are everywhere. Whether in a small isolated setting or a teeming metropolis, people have needs requiring the touch of God. Some are obvious. Some have become so commonplace they are unnoticed.

Mission opportunities exist for three reasons:

1. Some opportunities exist because local churches never see them. The needs may have existed in the community for a long time. However, without an intentional response from a caring church, these needs continue to go unmet. For example, an ex-neighborhood church whose members commute in to church from the suburbs might not be aware that a new community of Cambodian immigrants has located just two blocks away from the church.
2. Some opportunities exist because people have known about them but chosen not to respond to them. In the example above, a local church might be very aware that the Cambodians are nearby. However, the congregation might decide it does not have the resources to minister to a group of people whose culture is so different from their own.
3. Some opportunities exist because shifting populations and changing communities bring new people groups into the church's field of ministry. Many urban communities undergo ethnic transition as frequently as every ten years. Tomorrow's Kurdish population might replace today's Cambodian population.

Discovering mission opportunities can be as simple as taking a drive through the neighborhoods around the church. As you go, ask the following questions:

A. Where do the unreached groups of people live?
B. What racial, language, or cultural factors affect them? Are there any commercial signs that reflect a different culture or language group?
C. What physical and emotional challenges do they face? What is the condition of the housing stock? Is there any gang activity? Are there job opportunities nearby? Is there mass transit?
D. How do they spend their time? Are the people outside of their homes? What kind of music is predominant? Are the houses neatly landscaped and in good repair?

E. What are their socioeconomic needs? Are they rich? Middle income? Poor? Mixed?
F. What is their spiritual background? Are there any churches or other buildings in the community that reflect the spiritual background of the inhabitants?

Looking at a community with "missions eyes" will result in the discovery of many opportunities for evangelism, church planting, and ministry. Another way of discovering missions opportunities is to examine a demographic or psychographic report of the census tract(s) near your church. These tools will tell you about the age, income, race, education, household size, and lifestyles of the people living in the areas under investigation. Most local judicatories have access to these reports.

Once the church discovers its missions opportunities, it can prioritize them. The urgency of the needs, and the available resources with which to meet those needs, determine the ranking of each missions opportunity.

Develop Financial Resources

During the time that Cliff Temple faced a growing need for resources to fund the spiritual and charitable needs of the community, its own resources were rapidly declining. Contributions to the ministries budget of the church had declined at a steady rate of 15 percent per year throughout the 1980s. If fundamental changes were not made in its fund-raising practices, Cliff Temple would soon have no ministries.

It was out of this impending crisis that MISSION: Oak Cliff, Inc. was begun. It included both church and community leaders on its board of directors. Its only purpose for existing was to raise funds for the community ministries program of Cliff Temple.

The nonprofit corporation turned out to be a very important vehicle for resourcing Cliff Temple's missions ministries. We recognized that there were many people, charitable foundations, and organizations in the public sector interested in charitable and religious causes. However, because of restrictions or personal preference, they would not make contributions directly to a church. On the other hand, these same people gladly give to a separate nonprofit corporation that has no direct connection to an individual church.

By 1995, MISSION: Oak Cliff, Inc. was funding more than half the community ministries. By this time, the food pantry was serving more than seventeen thousand people, a threefold increase in three years. The clothing closet served half as many. Job training, English as a Second Language (ESL), summer lunch programs for school children, and holiday food and gift programs were added to the "mix" of community ministries. By 1999, the corporation was operating on a $175,000 budget and had added numerous much needed community ministries.

Meanwhile the church planting ministry networked with the community ministries program. Some mission churches received up to 50 percent funding through Baptist denominational channels. Most were self-supporting. Because of MISSION: Oak Cliff, the mission congregations did not have to concern themselves with developing a benevolence ministry of their own. Most were too small to be effective anyway. When some of the people in their church field had a need, they were sent to MISSION: Oak Cliff. The result was an effective, "synergizing" network of ministries.

Employ a Minister of Missions

Each church adopting the Key Church Strategy should employ a minister (or director) of missions to oversee the local church's missions program. The minister of missions can be a full-time, parttime, or volunteer, depending on the size, resources, and requirements of the particular church or denomination.

The Training, Function, and Job Description for the Minister of Missions

The minister (or director) of missions should come to the job with the education, background, and experience to affirm the position.

This person will be expected to take advantage of opportunities provided for continuing education.

The work of the minister of missions varies from church to church. In some churches, the minister of missions will be responsible for only the church planting ministry of the church. In other churches, the minister of missions may also be given the responsibility for community ministries, missions education and promotion, mission trips and/or evangelism.

There are four basic assignments common to the job descriptions of all Key Church ministers of missions:

1. The minister of missions is to give general administration to the missions program of the church.
2. The minister of missions is to enlist and train leadership for the church's missions program.
3. The minister of missions is to identify church planting opportunities and facilitate the birthing of new congregations.
4. The minister of missions is to develop a program of evangelism that will ensure every missions program and ministry to be evangelistic.

Whatever the specifics of the minister of missions' job description, he or she will need to do develop several skills to be successful in the ministry.

Develop leaders for ministry. The most critical need for any ministry is leadership. Without trained and committed leaders, the fruit of any missions ministry will be limited to the physical, emotional, and spiritual energy of the minister of missions. The successful minister of missions will learn quickly to multiply him or herself by training leaders who become his or her "hands and feet" in ministry.

Understand the difference between a leader and a worker. A worker is someone trained to perform a specific task. A worker may or may not be a leader. A leader is someone who attracts followers and develops them to their maximum effectiveness in ministry.

Recognize that two kinds of leaders are necessary for the successful implementation of the Key Church missions program. Administrative leaders work within the sponsor church to develop, promote, coordinate, and otherwise manage the program. Field leaders work primarily in the mission churches or ministries as pastors, project directors, or program directors.

Implement a Key Church Council. The Key Church Council is made up of all the church leaders who are involved in the missions program. As they work together, they will become a team that grows in expertise the longer they serve. Because they do not necessarily rotate on and off (as in a typical committee structure), the minister of missions should be careful about the people he or she enlists.

As the minister of missions develops the Key Church Council, he or she must carefully consider its size. It should be big enough to manage all of the mission and ministry projects of the church. Because the harvest is so plentiful, there is always the temptation to begin more new work than the sponsor church leadership can really support. The minister of missions may achieve impressive short-term results. However, if the support structure of the church is weak, the long-term future of the missions program may be in jeopardy.

Maintain communication with the pastor. The pastor of the church is ultimately the key to the success of the program. The minister of missions and the pastor should have enough rapport with each other that lines of communication are open and clear. The minister of missions must always support the pastor and his vision. The pastor must be aware and supportive of everything the minister of missions does. The minister of missions should constantly feed the pastor "hallelujah stories" that he can share with the congregation.

Develop a strategy for your program. The minister of missions must have a comprehensive vision for the church's missions program. While the vision begins at the local level, it must also include state, home, and foreign missions. Ministers of missions are not church planters—they are strategists who equip church planters.

Develop a strategy for the Key Church program. It is advisable to look at the many models currently in use. Two cautions are in order at this point. Do not be afraid to use others' models. If a model has been successful, glean from it the transferable principles and put them to use. Do not, however, fall into the trap of doing something a certain way just because another program does it that way.

Equip your workers. They are the hands and feet of the ministry. Give them initial and ongoing training. Mission pastors need to be trained for special services such as weddings, funerals, and the Lord's Supper. They will need to learn church planting and growth concepts, methods of evangelism and pastoral care, preaching, and administrative skills. They need to know how, when, and where to deliver their reports. Mission pastors should be encouraged to attend conferences or seminary extension for ongoing training.

Ministry leaders need to understand the basic methods of ministry. The larger regional judicatories and some of the smaller ones usually provide this kind of training for local churches.

Keep the church informed about your missions. One of the greatest challenges for the minister of missions is keeping the church informed about what is happening in the missions program. Most of the mission work is done off-campus. It is out of sight of the sponsor congregation and therefore "out of mind." Many people just do not understand why their church needs a missions program. Consequently, they need to be apprised of the many good things God is doing through the program. The effective minister of missions will make use of bulletin boards, the church newsletter and bulletin, presentations in Bible study classes, special worship services, and anything else he or she can think of to keep the missions program before the church.

Administer the program. Administering a church's local missions program is one of the most important jobs for the minister of missions. Worker enlistment, staff meetings, scheduling, budget development, and cost control are some of the responsibilities of the minister of missions. Meetings with the mission churches and regional judicatories will take up much the minister of missions' schedule.

Develop a system of report making and accountability. This system will include formal supervision for paid staff and some volunteers. For others, especially mission pastors, accountability is developed through a mentoring relationship. It is important to develop a reporting system reflecting appropriate levels of accountability.

The Enlistment of Volunteers

Enlisting volunteers is a critical part of the minister of missions' work. A new missions strategy may not have *any* volunteers with which to work. On the other hand, some of the leadership will already be in place. The Missions Auxiliary Directors, accustomed to working independently, will have to adjust to somewhat expanded roles on the Key Church Council. Most of the needed volunteers will come from the same pool of human resources from which the education, music, and evangelism ministries of the church have been fishing for some time. In most cases, this pool has been tapped out, leaving few, if any, committed volunteers.

Because he or she is working with a new strategy, the minister of missions needs some of the top volunteers of the church. The question then becomes, How does the minister of missions enlist needed volunteers without alienating other staff members or hurting existing church programs?

The answer is twofold. Before accepting the assignment, the minister of missions must negotiate with the church's decisio makers for permission to enlist top leadership to ensure the success of the mission program. Everyone in leadership, including staff, should be a part of the negotiations. Once permission is granted, the minister of missions should enlist the agreed upon personnel.

Once the initial volunteer leadership group is in place, the minister of missions should accept the responsibility to develop volunteers from among those who are not yet involved with other church programs. Some of these will be uninvolved church members. Others will be people yet to become church members. The minister of missions should adopt the maxim: "The resources are in the harvest."

Epilogue

The foundation laid at the beginning of the missions ministry of a Key Church determines the shape, strength, and longevity of the final product. The organization built upon the foundation will determine whether the Key Church Strategy is an integral part of the ministry of the church or merely an auxiliary to its work. The minister (or director) of missions the Key Church employs will also be a primary shaper of the future pattern of missions ministry for the church.

Tim Ahlen left Cliff Temple Baptist Church in 1995 after starting twenty-eight churches, several major community ministries and a 501(c)(3) corporation called MISSION: Oak Cliff, Inc. Because of the pattern developed in the first years of the Key Church Strategy, the ministry is still thriving and Cliff Temple is still a viable, vibrant force in a rapidly changing community.

3.

THE KEY CHURCH AND COMMUNITY MINISTRIES

Introduction

Any evangelistic strategy must ultimately be judged on how effectively people are reached and discipled. Good church growth *is* evangelistic growth. Good evangelistic growth is that which results in disciples, not just decisions. Twelve years into the strategy there was a lot of anecdotal evidence concerning the effectiveness of the Key Church Strategy. However, facts were needed.

In 1995, a questionnaire was mailed to Key Churches. A report was received from 212 churches, only 40 of which had been using the Key Church Strategy for more than three years. The Bible study attendance in those 40 Key Churches' satellite congregations totaled 33,807 that year. They baptized 6,616 new converts. Take this as an average over a three-year period: 19,848 persons were converted to Christ and baptized into the mission congregations. Nearly 59 percent of the Bible study attendance were newly baptized believers.

Taken together, all 212 Key Churches reported 20,123 baptisms in 1995. This is an average of 95 persons won to Christ and baptized per Key Church. In addition to churches planted, these Key Churches also started 398 new community ministries.

The 212 Key Churches are currently sponsoring 887 new mission churches. In 1995, the last year for which complete records are available, these churches started 262 new congregations. The average Key Church is sponsoring four congregations; two-thirds of these churches have been using the Key Church Strategy fewer than three years. This is effective evangelism. This is church growth!

Starting Churches by Meeting Needs

One Sunday morning, John Shelton, a layperson in his church, took his suburban youth group on a field trip to South Dallas to "show them what the inner city was like." He did not really know in advance where he was going, but when he got there, he knew he had arrived. It was a vacant lot deep in one of the roughest neighborhoods in South Dallas.

The only things on the lot were a couple of trees and a rusted out fifty-five-gallon drum. Because it was a cool morning, a half-dozen or so homeless persons had lit a fire in the barrel and were standing around it to warm themselves.

When he spotted them, he stopped his vehicle and said to the youth, "Here we are. Let's go!" He led them the short distance across the field. As he approached the people standing around the barrel, one of them walked toward him. He said to John, "What you doing here, white boy? Don't you know where you are?" John replied, "I know exactly why I'm here. God sent me to share his Word with you." John began to share the love of God with those men and women. The crowd grew. Half an hour later, more than twenty homeless people (drunks, crack addicts, prostitutes, and people just down on their luck) were standing around that barrel. They were now holding hands with John and his youth, praying for strength, mercy, and salvation from the only one who could provide it—the Lord Jesus Christ.

Over the next several weeks and months, John found himself drawn repeatedly back to the lot. Each week, he would come with nothing but his Bible and a knapsack full of oranges. He searched out needy people who were living on the streets or in burned out or condemned buildings. He gave them an orange, put his arms around them, prayed for them, and invited them to his worship service on the lot.

The ministry grew until it became more than one person could do on his own. John needed some sponsorship. After a number of prayerful discussions, the Cliff Temple Baptist Church agreed to give him the support he needed. We decided to call his ministry "Church on the Lot."

Over the intervening months, the worship service on the vacant lot grew until it was attracting more than one hundred persons each week. In addition to the weekly worship services, John and his helpers also set up Sidewalk Sunday Schools at several of the neighborhood apartment complexes. Week after week, they introduced people to the life-changing love of Christ.

Soon there was a need for a facility to house people trying to put their lives back together. At this point, the Dallas Baptist Association and Baptist General Convention stepped in to provide the support needed to open the East Dallas Outreach Center. The Center provides a safe haven for homeless people in need of a shower, a meal, or a place to rest. It provides support and housing for people who are serious about turning their lives around. It provides access to health care, counseling, and job training so desperately needed by the residents. A women's center is currently being established in the Oak Cliff section of Dallas. It will provide for the same needs as the East Dallas center. It will also provide childcare, crisis pregnancy counseling, and abuse counseling.

The Church on the Lot has reproduced itself through several apartment ministries and the establishment of Oasis Baptist Church. Each of these congregations shares the same commitment to ministry as its sponsor church. Indeed, Church on the Lot remains the anchor church for the many congregations.

The Church on the Lot is a significant part of the Key Church story. Like Mission Arlington, which will be discussed later in this book, its people are committed to evangelizing and making congregations of people as they meet physical, emotional, and spiritual needs in the name of Christ. They reach out to people who do not fit into the programs and strategies of traditional churches. They reach out to people who are very close to the heart of our Lord.

"Then the righteous will answer him, 'Lord, when did we see you hungry and feed you, or thirsty and give you something to drink? When did we see you a stranger and invite you in, or needing clothes and clothe you? When did we see you sick or in prison and go to visit you?' The King will reply, 'I tell you the truth, whatever you did for one of the least of these brothers of mine, you did for me.' " (Matthew 25:37-40)

Evangelism Through Community Ministry

Community ministry takes many forms. In low-income, distressed communities, community ministry will be to the "down and outers." Emergency services like food, clothing, shelter, and refuge will meet immediate needs. Empowerment ministries such as job training, English language, parenting and life skills training help prevent recurrence of the emergencies. Higher income communities have their share of emergencies needing Christian ministry. Losses of work, divorce, death, foreclosure, and other financial distress affect the "up and outers" as much as they do the "down and outers." When people are unaccustomed to struggling with failure in life, the needs might be even greater. Likewise, empowerment ministries for the professional classes are essential. Parenting, interpersonal skill development, debt management, and other life management skills are needed for this group.

No matter which group a Key Church targets, beginning and growing churches by meeting people at the point of their needs is a very effective means of outreach. In order for this approach to be effective, there are several issues to consider.

Theological Motivations for Community Ministry

There are many people and organizations providing for community needs. Most of these help people in an adequate way. People do not have to come to a church to find assistance in meeting their needs. However, the church does provide some unique dimensions as it practices community ministry. One of these is the theological motivation we have for serving people. Our motivation for service is perhaps the most striking characteristic that makes our community ministry different from the social services provided by secular agencies. That motivation comes from our own compassion, which, in turn, finds its source in God's love for all human beings. We serve in grateful obedience to God's will. This motivation is a result of some basic theological truths:

- People are the highest creation of God with infinite potential and value and as such are of infinite worth.
- People are whole beings made up of physical, emotional, and spiritual segments that cannot be separated or isolated.
- God desires the highest good for all people, which is life in fellowship with him on earth and in his eternal kingdom.
- People are motivated to serve by God's love for him and by the love of God as revealed in his Son, Jesus Christ.

Principles for Practicing Community Ministry

The motivation previously mentioned should lead us to the following principles to guide us as we seek to meet the needs of individuals. Because every person is created by God and is of infinite value, no one should be excluded in our attempt to minister. Some Christians have been guilty of judging persons as either "worthy" or "unworthy" of our help. There is no such thing as an "unworthy" person. The fact that God created each person makes anyone worthy of our help.

1. Because people are free agents, we must allow each person the right to make his or her own decisions. We must allow each person to take care of himself or herself as much as possible. This means we can make suggestions, but we must never force our solution on someone else. It means that we take the time to discover what persons can do for themselves and allow them to do as much as they can. We have a tendency to want to take control of a situation too quickly.

2. Because people are whole, and because God desires the highest good for all persons, we are concerned with all

aspects of a person's well-being. Not only do we meet his or her physical need, but we also seek to meet his or her emotional and spiritual needs. Community ministry and evangelism go hand in hand.

Qualities for Practicing Community Ministry

A person must have certain qualities if he or she is to be effective in community ministry.

1. *Warmth.* This quality refers to the part of a person's personality that identifies his or her humanness. He or she is able to have an attitude of friendliness, respect, and an appreciation for the other person's worth. He or she genuinely cares about the other person.
2. *Empathy.* This means the minister can feel with and understand the other person, not just intellectually, but emotionally. The empathetic minister can feel the pain of another, but does not reside in it and is not incapacitated by it.
3. *Authenticity.* The minister must be genuine. He cannot prattle or use an assumed smile. These come across as phony.

Dangers in Practicing Community Ministry

There are some pitfalls or dangers to be aware of and guard against as one practices community ministry.

1. *Helping others in order to meet personal needs.* Ministers must not simply try to get the person in need to change his or her behavior in order to please the minister. The minister must not become angry because the person in need does not do what the minister wants or progress at the rate he or she would like.
2. *Playing the role of rescuer.* The rescuing minister constantly bails out a person in need, though sometimes it may be better not to do so. Persons in need should be taught to solve their own problems if possible. If they know how to solve

their problems and choose not to, the minister's attempt to rescue will only serve to prolong the problem.

3. *The Messiah syndrome.* The minister suffering from Messiah syndrome does not realize his limitations or those of his church. The minister's own need to fix the problem can become an obsession that ignores principles of good stewardship and ministry.

4. *Being the final authority.* This person believes he or she has all the answers and tries to force those answers on the person who is seeking help.

The Person in Need

There are four major reasons a person seeks help. It is important to understand these reasons so the right action can be taken to assist the person.

1. *Something within the person is inadequate to remove or cope with the problem.* Physical challenges or mental or emotional limitations sometimes make it necessary for a community agency like a church to intervene. In these instances, the church needs to look at both short- and long-term solutions to the problem.

2. *Environmental conditions are working against the person.* For example, a jobless person may live in a community where there are limited opportunities for employment. The community may not have public transportation, making travel to and from work difficult or impossible for people without private transportation.

3. *Inflexible rules, practices, or laws.* Immigration laws make people from other countries ineligible for most governmental assistance. However, the children of illegal aliens become just as hungry as those of fifth-generation Americans if there is no food in the house. The church is usually the only community agency that can give humanitarian assistance without being hampered by government restrictions.

4. *Accidents or disasters.* These are the most common situa-

tions encountered by churches' community ministries programs. Sudden losses of income or shelter, or spouse or child
abuse, can be overcome by timely and proper intervention by
a caring church.

Steps to Ministering to Persons in Need

There are some basic steps to take to help a person in need.
These are simply guidelines and are not set in concrete. They give
one a direction in which to go when dealing with persons in need.
The minister always needs to depend on the leadership of the
Holy Spirit when making final decisions about a course of action.

The Assessment Stage

This is the stage when one tries to discover the needs of the person seeking help. There are three parts to this stage:

1. *Information gathering.* Find out as much about the person
   and his problem as possible. Develop a detailed questionnaire that asks for personal information such as name,
   address, date of birth, Social Security number, driver's
   license number, employment, marital status, total number of
   people living in the home and their names, whether they are
   currently receiving governmental assistance, and who else
   they have talked to about their problem.
2. *Perceived needs.* Find out what the person believes his or her
   needs are, and what he or she feels is the best way to deal
   with them. It is vital to allow the other person to express his
   or her view and have a say in the decisions being made. During this phase, the interviewer should also ask how many
   times the person has had this problem before. Write all
   responses on the interview questionnaire.
3. *Existing Assets.* Discover what assets the client possesses
   that may be used to help solve the problem. Assets include
   cash, property, skills, family, and friends. Most people coming to a church for assistance will have some assets that can
   be used to help solve the problem.

The Intervention Stage

This stage is where the minister attempts to meet the person's needs. There are two areas of need to address.

1. *The immediate need.* Immediate needs include things like shelter, food, safety, and work. If appropriate and possible, the church can meet the need. In this case, the assistance provided is direct and immediate. If it is beyond the church's capacity to provide immediate assistance, refer the person to an appropriate agency. Most cities have an agency serving as a clearinghouse for referrals. A directory is frequently published which lists all the social service agencies in a city, what services they provide, hours of operation, and qualifications for receiving aid. When making referrals, never promise something for another agency or church!

2. *Chronic needs.* Options should also be discussed with the person for keeping this need from becoming or continuing to be chronic. The person must decide for himself or herself what steps he or she will take, but options must be presented first. Discuss the ensuing consequences with each alternative.

The Follow-up Stage

Whenever possible, the minister should make follow-up contact with the persons in need to see how they are progressing and to show a sincere interest in their well-being. It is at this stage that evangelistic efforts can be most effective. The minister should tell the persons seeking help upfront that he or she cares for both their spiritual and physical well-being. Let them know that you or someone from your church, or one of your mission churches, will be visiting them soon. Follow through on that. It is as important to present Jesus to them unashamedly as it is to present food or a check for their rent. Follow-up will also allow the minister to discover if further assistance may be needed or sought by the person.

Which Community Ministries?

The range of possible community ministries is as wide as the range of human need. Deciding which ones are appropriate for a particular church requires careful assessment.

1. Determine if a particular need is widespread enough to warrant the beginning of a new ministry. If the church is in transition to a primarily Hispanic or Asian neighborhood, chances are there will be a need for English as a Second Language (ESL) classes. If the church is in a new subdivision that is 100 percent Anglo or African American, ESL is not going to be worth the effort. If the church's neighborhood has 10 percent or more of its people living in poverty, a food pantry will likely be needed in the community. If the average price of homes in the neighborhood of the church is $250,000, emergency food will not likely be a high priority.

2. Discover whether another church or agency in the community is already meeting the particular need. As long as the level of quality service in a particular area is adequate, there is no need for starting a new ministry. If no one else is meeting a particular need, or if the agency providing the service has no Christian emphasis to it, then it is appropriate for the Key Church to consider starting a ministry designed to meet the need.

3. Discover the resources and permits needed to begin the ministry. Resources include money, volunteers, and facilities, all of which will be needed to conduct the ministry. Permits may be required by the local health department for a food pantry or other food distribution ministry. There may be an application necessary to participate with the local food bank. To be sure, there will never be enough resources; the Lord of the harvest said that! (Matthew 9:37-38). Still, it is important to have sufficient resources so that the ministry will be successful.

Once these three steps are followed, it will be clearer which community ministries your church can become involved in. There will be an unmet human need for which your church has the available resources to fulfill.

Resources for Community Ministry

The Cliff Temple Baptist Church of Dallas, Texas, employed its first minister of benevolent ministries in 1948, making it one of the first Southern Baptist churches to give staff status to community ministries. Over the next forty years, the benevolent ministry program grew in importance in the church, both in terms of the membership's commitment to it, and in terms of the community's growing need for emergency and empowerment services. At its zenith, the ministry, known as the Care Center, employed two full-time and one part-time staff members. It ran a number of very effective programs including a food pantry, clothing closet, meals on wheels, special food and gift programs for Thanksgiving and Christmas seasons, ESL and GED classes, immigration assistance, and a Mothers Club designed to give life skills training to newly immigrated Hispanic mothers.

As the effects of ethnic transition progressed, the church found itself in the unenviable position to try to meet increasing needs with precipitously declining human and financial resources. By the time Tim Ahlen began work there as minister of missions in 1992, the church was able to budget only $7,200 per year for the entire benevolent ministry. Designated gifts added another $15,000 per year, but these gifts had been declining 15 percent per year for the last decade. Where the program had at one time boasted three paid staff members, it now had one-third of a paid staff member's job description and about 100 highly committed, but aging, volunteers. The median age of the church's membership was 72.

The big question the church had to face was, How are we going to develop resources that will be sufficient in the years ahead to meet the increasing human needs of the people living in Oak Cliff? The immediate response was both understandable and unrealistic. The lay leadership of the church basically said, "Well, we'll just have to work a little harder, get a few more volunteers from the church, and get them to give to the program."

The answer was not simply to work a little harder. The church had to work differently. The solution the church came up with was to turn the Care Center ministry from a single church ministry into a church and community partnership. Cliff Temple established a community-based nonprofit corporation called MISSION: Oak Cliff, Inc. The purpose of the corporation was to develop funding to staff and provide operating funds for the programs the Oak Cliff community desperately needed. The board of directors was made up of a combination of Cliff Temple members and some shakers and movers from the community. To raise funds, the organization targeted charitable and religious foundations, corporations, and individuals who had a concern for community ministry but could not, or would not, give to a single church.

Within three years, MISSION: Oak Cliff, Inc. was bringing in more than $150,000 in outside grants. They were able to add two part-time staff members. The Care Center food ministry grew from eight thousand people served annually to more than twenty-two thousand people served annually. MISSION: Oak Cliff began several satellite food pantries in South Oak Cliff. They provided a summer lunch program for underprivileged children, a literacy program for English speakers, and a number of other programs.

With the explosive growth in services provided, the organization ran into a second resource challenge—where do we get the volunteers to run the programs? Traditionally, all of the volunteers came from Cliff Temple members and a close circle of their friends. As mentioned above, these folks were highly dedicated but getting older and beginning to run out of gas. The average age of volunteers when Ahlen began work at Cliff Temple was almost eighty. The oldest volunteer was ninety-eight! Many of them had been volunteering for twenty years or more. As the ministry grew, the leaders recognized that there were no more willing people to call on to be volunteers.

The only choice was to look to the community for assistance. They began to ask some of the members of nearby mission churches to volunteer. They asked some of our former clients to help. It didn't take long for the Care Center volunteer staff to begin taking on the complexion of the community. These changes were some of the most difficult for the church to deal with, but not because of the racial differences between the old volunteers and the new. Rather, it was because the older volunteers felt that the ministry was being taken away from the people who had devoted the later years of their lives to developing it. Nonetheless, the community became a vital resource for people to run the community ministry program.

Facility resources were never a problem for Cliff Temple's community ministries program. The primary facility was an old converted house called the Goslin Building. Named for the church's first minister of benevolence ministries, it was owned and maintained by the church. It housed the church's food pantry and clothing closet, and served as the hub of the other community activities. Educational and other programs were given space in Cliff Temple's main building. Satellite food pantries were opened in donated buildings and apartments throughout Oak Cliff and South Dallas. Of the three kinds of resources, facilities were the easiest to develop.

Epilogue

People sometimes wonder how much impact "giveaway" programs can have in changing people's lives. One day Tim Ahlen was leading a regional church growth conference, sharing the story of Church on the Lot. As he finished his presentation, he admitted that many, if not most, of the people who made professions of faith in Christ through that ministry continued to struggle with alcohol, drugs and other destructive lifestyles. As he finished, a man named Chuck Stevenson raised his hand in the back of the auditorium and said, "Wait a minute! That's not the end of the story!" Chuck went on to say that he lived in Irving, Texas, and that his son, who lived out of town, was traveling in Dallas when his car broke down just off the freeway in a dangerous part of South Dallas. He called his dad to come and help him fix the broken down car. When Chuck arrived, he noticed a man standing across the street watching them. It made them nervous, so they worked a little faster. The sun began going down, and the stranger across the street continued to watch them. Just as it turned dark, the man began to walk toward them. "I've been watching you," he said as he came up alongside their car.

"We know," Chuck and his son replied very nervously.

"Well, this is not a very safe place for people to be this time of day, and I just wanted to make sure nobody bothered you." The man offered his help, and soon they had completed the repair.

As they finished up, Chuck decided to be brave and talk to the man about his faith. He asked him if he went to church. The man said, "Oh yes, Brother John is my pastor. I go to Church on the Lot!" That issue taken care of, the man asked Chuck if he would be so kind as to drive him home. Feeling so much better about the man who had been watching them so carefully, he agreed. He followed the man's directions, and finally the man said, "Stop here."

Chuck looked to his left and his right and, seeing no house nearby, he said, "Where do you live?"

"Oh," this Christian said, "I live right there, up in that tree!" Imagine—foxes have holes, and birds have nests; but right in the middle of Dallas, Texas, there is one man living in a tree who learned how to be Christlike through a church wholly devoted to community ministry.

4.

HANG OUT AND HOVER

AN INDIGENOUS SATELLITE STRATEGY

HANG OUT ON PROPERTY AND HOVER
AROUND JOHN 3:16

A phone call came to Tillie by way of the custodian of the church. A lady needed help. Tillie went to an apartment. She had never been to a place quite like that. The lady's electricity was going to be turned off if she didn't get some help. There was a physical need. Tillie got some help for her and asked, "Can we have a Bible study in your apartment?" "Oh, Ms. Tillie, I don't even have any furniture in my apartment. I've never had a Bible study in my home!" The next Sunday, seventeen people from that apartment community met in her apartment, and many, for the first time, heard about God's unconditional love.

Not long after that, Tillie met another lady, Virginia, who was in need. Tillie talked with her about her needs and promised to stop by her apartment with some groceries. When Tillie arrived, she found an empty apartment. Tillie saw to it that the electric bill was paid—with her own money. Just before leaving, Tillie said, "Would it be all right if we had a Bible study here?"

"Here?" Virginia responded. Tillie said, "Why not?" That Bible study grew to sixty people. It became a church in the true sense. These were rough, tough kinds of folks—like the people Jesus preached to—and they weren't about to come to church. We decided to take the church to them, which is what He did.

Virginia Maanani joined in and was immediately looked up to as a leader because the Bible Study was in her home. She grew in her faith rapidly, and soon found people coming to her for answers to their spiritual problems. She never asked to be a spiritual leader; it just happened. She seemed to understand her neighbors and the problems they encountered on a daily basis. She could relate to the residents in ways that a professional minister never could.

The case has already been made for using the indigenous principle in local mission work. However, when applied in the context of starting lower-income, single-cell churches, it is important to recognize that the sponsoring church still plays a major support role for the new congregation. In planetary science, the sun is the center of the solar system. Planets surround the sun as satellites. The sun is gaseous; the planets are mostly made up of solids and liquids. Planets are different from the sun. They have an identity of their own. Yet, they are dependent on the sun for their heat and light. Without the sun, our own planet would die. In the same way, when a church plants satellite churches in multifamily housing communities or in densely populated urban areas, the new congregations are dependent on the sponsor church. With its support, these congregations, called Indigenous Satellite Churches, thrive; without strong support of a sponsor church, they die.

The strategy of planting Indigenous Satellite Churches preceded the Key Church Strategy. It has been a method of helping churches to see church starting from a positive point of view. It can be done without costing large amounts of money. The churches can be planted and developed with lay pastors. It can be done without losing members from the Key Church's congregation. It accelerates growth. It is a very effective evangelism strategy!

An Indigenous Satellite Church (ISC) is a single-cell church that remains a permanent part of the sponsoring church. The purpose of the ISC is to reach and disciple non-Christians and other unchurched people. An Indigenous Satellite congregation is self-supporting, self-governing, self-multiplying, and shares the culture in which it is planted.

The Indigenous Satellite Strategy utilizes an effective method of evangelism. Through it, a local church reaches new people within their own socioeconomic, language, and cultural groups. The method builds bridges to other groups of people that may never be reached by the church with the usual, single congregation.

The principles of starting and operating an Indigenous Satellite Church are the same as for a more traditional church that is to be constituted into an independent church. However, the unique application of those principles is what makes the Indigenous Satellite Strategy so successful. There are at least ten reasons to use the Indigenous Satellite Strategy.

1. Accelerates Growth

The Indigenous Satellite Church Strategy accelerates growth because these missions can be started with a limited amount of leadership and financial help from the home church.

The Cliff Temple Baptist Church in Dallas, Texas, ran eight hundred in average attendance in satellite congregations with only fourteen persons from the home church active in mission leadership. The Coulter Road Baptist Church in Amarillo, Texas, started an Indigenous Satellite Church in a manufactured home park. Within six months, eight persons had been baptized. Pastor Travis LaDuke described the work as "the best stewardship of our members. We reached more people for Christ, per worker enlisted in the mobile home park, than any ministry of our church."[1]

Two or three laypersons are enough to send out from the home church to start an Indigenous Satellite Church. The laypersons need to be taught how to reach and disciple people in the community so that they become leaders in the core group. Too many persons coming from the sponsoring church can prove to be negative because this moves away from the indigenous mission principle. It is more positive for two or three persons to communicate the gospel, win persons to Christ, and begin the work with the new, or previously inactive, Christians. When there is a core group of six to twenty-five adults, a pastor can be called from resources out of the group.

A new Indigenous Satellite Church congregation can be started by enlisting and supporting one bivocational pastor. Commonly, when the new work is started by enlisting a bivocational pastor, no families are needed from the sponsoring Key Church. The pastor frequently has a network of people he or she can enlist as core group members. If not, he or she can visit in the community to find, disciple, and develop new and inactive Christians into a core group to start the new Indigenous Satellite Church.

A new Indigenous Satellite Church congregation can also be started with a volunteer layperson serving as pastor. Starting with a lay pastor is especially effective when planting a working-class Anglo, ethnic, or foreign language congregation. The pastor needs to be of the same ethnicity as the target group. It is much easier for a person to discover, enlist, and disciple persons of his or her own ethnicity. Working-class persons prefer a pastor who knows how to work with his or her hands.

The need for new Indigenous Satellite Church congregations may not be obvious. Many times an ethnic or language group can be invisible to the average church member. One way of identifying the need for a foreign language congregation is to check with the local school system. Most urban areas will be home to between seventy-five and one hundred distinct language groups.

Among those groups whose primary language is not English, a large population base is not needed to start a healthy congregation. Ethnic persons are easier to congregate when they represent a very small percent of the population in the community. Events focused toward them, within the context of their culture, become very attractive. Most persons in this environment become hungry for fellowship with people from their home culture. Friendships can be quickly made, and the Indigenous Satellite Church provides a social as well as spiritual reinforcement. It is possible to reach entire groups with new Indigenous Satellite Churches. It is common for 75 to 80 percent of the entire population to be reached with a new Indigenous Satellite congregation, in a short time, because of the cultural pull. Reaching ethnic groups becomes very cost-effective because large numbers of people can be reached with a small number of people, and with limited financial resources.

Financial resources come from the new persons who are reached through a new Indigenous Satellite Church. This is the basis of the adage: "The resources are in the harvest."

2. Easy Site Selection

The Indigenous Satellite Church has many options in the selection of a place to meet for Bible study and worship. Adult Sunday school department rooms make an excellent place to meet. Other places to meet could be homes, rented houses, mobile chapels, apartments, multihousing club rooms, theaters, store fronts, or other church buildings. Several Indigenous Satellite Churches can meet in one building. One very effective place to start a new Indigenous Satellite Church targeting middle-class persons is a restaurant. A private room in a restaurant is ideal for the core group meeting. It is easy to find, food service is available, and, in some cases, can be expanded as the group grows. Hotels provide even more options. Conference rooms can be added to provide space for a new developing congregation.

Flexibility is the key word in the selection of meeting places for Indigenous Satellite Churches. Be ready to move as needed. The new people attending need to be included in decisions about meeting places. The geographical location is not as important as one might think. The class of persons being contacted for the new Indigenous Satellite congregation will determine the kind of people reached, not the geographical location of the meeting place. Still, the meeting place should reflect the cultural values of the particular group of people being targeted.

3. Ideal for Multifamily Housing Ministry

The Indigenous Satellite Church Strategy can be used to reach people living in multifamily housing. In fact, it was the first effective strategy to reach multihousing communities. In the past, most ministries to apartment dwellers have been designed to get people to leave the complex, and attend the services in the church's buildings. Very few have been successful. The Indigenous Satellite Church ministry allows you to get inside the community with the gospel, disciple the residents, and encourage them to establish their own church meeting inside their community.

Other multifamily housing strategies have involved a large expenditure of human effort and finances. Some have been very successful, but when the ministry was concluded, the people being reached became inactive. The ministry continued only as long as the efforts were being made by the sponsoring church or churches. The Indigenous Satellite Strategy is effective in the multifamily housing environment because of its indigenous methodology. The people in the community take ownership. The church becomes *their* church! When the people who started the work no longer participate, the residents continue because it is *their* church. When an Indigenous Satellite Church is started, it will continue as long as the residents want it.

Multihousing communities are the largest mission field in America today. The Indigenous Satellite Church Strategy is an effective means of reaching them for Christ.

4. Heterogeneous Churches Develop

The Indigenous Satellite Church ministry offers a church the opportunity to become heterogeneous, rather than homogeneous. Most churches are homogeneous. In other words, most of the members are from the same cultural background. Most communities in America are heterogeneous. That is, they are made up of many cultures. Charles Lee Williamson, in his book *Growing Your Church in Seven Days,* says, "People congregate with similar people. People tend to congregate across one-third of the socio-economic spectrum. Most churches will find that approximately half of its congregation is positioned on one rung on the scale." He uses an arbitrary scale of 1 to 9. The low end of the scale represents people who live below the poverty line and/or are functionally illiterate. The high end of the scale represents people making in excess of $100,000 per year and/or have earned doctoral degrees. He goes on to say, "Another 40 percent is divided evenly on the two rungs on both sides of the 50 percent rung. The remaining 10 percent can be found anywhere on the spectrum. The average church finds a socioeconomic niche that represents approximately one-third of the community from which it draws members."[2]

The homogeneous unit principle is a practical one to utilize in church planting. However, it contradicts the biblical teaching that Jesus Christ died for *all* people. The single congregational homogeneous church, by nature, excludes all people who are different from the dominant group in the church. The Indigenous Satellite Church Strategy, on the other hand, establishes numerous homogeneous cells bonded together by their common bond with the sponsor church. Thus, it is an excellent method for producing heterogeneous churches. It allows the church to become as heterogeneous as the community by having homogeneous Indigenous Satellite Church congregations as functioning parts of the sponsor church.

5. Develops Indigenous Leadership

The Indigenous Satellite Church Strategy makes it possible to develop indigenous leadership from the community. A person with an eighth-grade education may not be able to serve as the adult Bible teacher in a church made up of business and other professional people. However, he or she could be a strong leader in an Indigenous Satellite Church made up of others with an eighth-grade education.

A Spanish-speaking person can't be a leader in an English-speaking church, but he or she could be very effective in a Spanish-speaking Indigenous Satellite church. Each person is encouraged to reach his or her highest potential for developing leadership skills when the options become available through the ISC strategy. There is a place for every potential leader.

Just as resources come from the harvest of the unsaved and unchurched, leadership comes from the harvest of evangelism.

The most effective leaders are those from the community who have been reached for Christ, discipled, and trained while serving in the new church.

6. Reproduces Rapidly

The Indigenous Satellite Church ministry allows a church to experience accelerated growth because an Indigenous Satellite Church can be established immediately and can multiply rapidly without the lengthy amount of time and financial commitment required by the traditional approach. Churches using this strategy don't have to wait! The church can expand when and where God opens doors. Many Key Churches have been able to double their attendance in fewer than three years because of this. This means they are quickly able to reach as many outside as they do within the walls of the traditional church.

Rapid reproduction is the reason the church grew so explosively in the New Testament era. The barriers related to buildings and land faced by traditional churches today were not present in the New Testament churches.

7. Maximizes Community Penetration

The Indigenous Satellite Church ministry can provide churches for new people living in geographically churched areas. Traditionally, a community is considered "churched" if numerous church buildings are located in the community—although only a small percentage of the population may attend church on any given Sunday! This view of assessing the need for new churches is the reason church growth has not kept pace with population growth. In communities where new churches have been started, there is not a negative impact on the attendance of the established churches. However, there has been a very positive impact on the total number of persons in church attendance on the average Sunday.

The truth is that the more evangelistic churches in a community, the more people attend. Where there are fewer churches, fewer people attend church. While there are some significant exceptions, most traditional churches begin to decrease in their growth rate, or stop growing altogether, when they are ten or more years old. New churches are needed in order to penetrate the population and reach more people for Christ.

The penetration into a community's population would be the same if the church became one church with many congregations as it would if new independent churches were started.

Most churches have groups of people who are unsaved living near their buildings. Many times these unsaved persons are culturally removed from the people who regularly worship in the community. A new Indigenous Satellite Church, created with these dissimilar groups of people and targeted with the gospel, can be very effective in evangelizing and discipling them.

8. Overcomes Resistance to New Churches

The Indigenous Satellite Church overcomes the resistance of established churches to new churches. Many church leaders view starting a new church as competition! The growth and expansion of an established church is viewed with appreciation. The Indigenous Satellite Church Strategy allows established churches to start new churches within the fellowship and structure of their own church. Other churches will view the starting of Indigenous Satellite Church congregations as a positive ministry, whereas the starting of new, traditional churches is often viewed negatively. The new Indigenous Satellite Church is viewed as a ministry, rather than competition, because it targets the persons the established churches are unable to reach.

The ISC Strategy also allows the sponsoring Key Churches to reach beyond their immediate geographical area with a ministry of evangelism and extension and without major resistance. This strategy makes it possible to reach into new suburban housing communities, wherever they are, and at the same time reach into the inner city and ethnic communities within the area. This evangelistic mission outreach will be viewed by other established churches with appreciation because it is an expanding ministry to the unchurched. The purpose is not to take members from established churches. This strategy can be equitably accomplished through cooperation with other churches.

9. Maximizes Use of Existing Space

The Indigenous Satellite Church ministry makes it possible to start ministries in and around the sponsoring churches' buildings. There is more unused floor space in America's churches than in any other institution. Churches have primarily constructed single-use facilities designed for Bible study and worship. This space is chiefly used on Sunday mornings, and large portions go unused Sunday afternoon and evening. Almost all of the space is unused during the remainder of the week. No other organization or industry could afford this waste of resources! It is not good stewardship of Kingdom assets.

Hundreds of Indigenous Satellite Church congregations could be using these buildings. The only thing necessary here is to convince church leaders that their church must respond to people's needs. People will congregate around the solution to their felt needs. The needs will be different among various individuals and people groups. Where people meet is not nearly as important as what happens in the meeting and with whom they meet.

The Indigenous Satellite Church Strategy maximizes the use of the unused space in America's church buildings. These structures are designed for worship and Bible study, and this is the primary focus of the Indigenous Satellite Church Strategy.

Unchurched persons, when discipled, will attend church at different times and in different places than traditional Christians attending traditional churches. This opens many avenues for use of church buildings. The buildings can be used many times on Sunday and every day of the week for Bible study, worship, and diverse ministry activities.

The following is a limited list of illustrations for the use of church buildings:

1. Several Indigenous Satellite Churches can use sponsoring church buildings at alternative times.

2. Social ministries can be coupled with an evangelism strategy that allows a new Indigenous Satellite Church to be started from the ministry.
3. An Indigenous Satellite Church meeting across from the sponsoring church building is not viewed negatively because it is still one church.
4. Ministry for adult nonreaders.
5. Ministry with deaf people.
6. Ministry with homeless people.
7. Ministry with immigrants.
8. Ministry in the afternoons for latchkey children.
9. Ministry with substance abusers.
10. Food distribution.

10. Promotes Church Planting for the Poor

The Indigenous Satellite Church ministry is a way to evangelize, minister, and start new mission church congregations for the poor and working-class population.

Ask any church member if churches are concerned about the poor in the community. The answer will overwhelmingly be "yes!" This question was asked of a suburban congregation in the Dallas area recently, and the entire group answered in the affirmative.

The quick response of church members to express interest in the needs of the poor perhaps is the result of the strong admonition of the Bible. The psalmist says that God blesses those who are kind to the poor (Psalm 41:1).

A survey of the Texas population completed in 1974 showed that 80 percent of the unchurched families were poor and working class. Recent surveys, especially those targeting lower-income, multifamily housing communities, show that about 90 percent of the poor are unchurched.[3]

The missions division director at that time, Charles Lee Williamson, said many times, "The greatest mission field in Texas is the poor and working-class population."[4] James Palmer, chairman of the Sociology Department at East Texas Baptist University, states, "Social participation studies have consistently shown that lower-class people join few associations, even the church." He further states, "The lower-class person will have most of his relationships, outside of work, with members of his own family, and with very close neighbors."[5]

It is difficult to determine why the poor are not represented in the evangelical churches in proportion to their population in the community. The problem is that it is difficult to measure the apathy, alienation, resentment, and lack of welcome the poor may have experienced. There is a need for churches to reconsider their relationship and responsibilities to the poor.

The Indigenous Satellite Church Strategy has been the major strategy for successfully reaching the poor and working class. The First Baptist Church of Arlington, Texas, has made this their major strategy, and each week approximately three thousand poor and working-class persons are engaged in Bible study and worship in over two hundred Indigenous Satellite congregations. The church begins the satellite ministry by providing food, clothing, furniture, help with rent and utility bills, counseling, and health care through medical clinics staffed by medical professionals.

The First Baptist Church of Dallas, Texas, has given priority to the poor and working class through their Indigenous Satellite Church ministry. The Dallas Life Foundation provides food, clothing, and help with securing jobs, as well as Bible study and worship for approximately four hundred street persons each day. The people reached through their chapels are primarily of the poor and working class.

These two illustrations are examples of what many Key Churches are doing across the nation. Of the 396 new ministries created in 1995 by 212 Key Churches, most targeted the poor and working class.

There are at least seven reasons the Indigenous Satellite Church Strategy so effectively reaches the poor:

1. Poor and working-class persons seek relationships in small groups! The Indigenous Satellite congregations can be small, and many of them can be started in order to reach large numbers through many small congregations.

2. Poor and working-class persons do not typically join many formal organizations! The informal, indigenous structure of the ISC congregations is inviting to such individuals.
3. Poor and working-class persons are family centered! The ISC can minister to the whole family. Relationship evangelism, which reaches out to the extended family, is a good ISC strategy.
4. Poor and working-class persons have a very low trust level! The ISC strategy is an indigenous missions strategy. Leaders come from within the ISC congregation so that leadership is given to persons the congregation trusts.
5. Many poor and working-class persons have conservative values. This means they are also religious conservatives. Bible study and preaching can be presented from a conservative perspective.
6. Poor and working-class persons often have a low educational level. All activities need to be presented at an appropriate educational level. This can be done in an ISC. It cannot be done if everyone is asked to come to one place at one time.
7. Poor and working-class persons do not always have the kinds of clothes to wear that would make them comfortable in many middle-class churches. They can dress in what they have in an ISC belonging to them.

In conclusion, the Indigenous Satellite Strategy is a proven way for churches to reach all kinds of people, in all kinds of places, and at all different times. It is the most flexible church growth strategy available today. It allows the church to follow the biblical example of the apostle Paul:

> To the Jews I became like a Jew, to win the Jews. To those under the law I became like one under the law (though I myself am not under the law), so as to win those under the law. To those not having the law I became like one not having the law (though I am not free from God's law but am under Christ's law), so as to win those not having the law. To the weak I became weak, to win the weak. I have become all things to all men so that by all possible means I might save some. I do all this for the sake of the gospel, that I may share in its blessings. (1 Corinthians 9:20-23)

Epilogue

One Sunday morning, tragedy struck in Virginia's apartment community. A baby had died. As soon as Tillie Burgin heard about the death, she went over to the community to see what she could do. She knew that the family was poor and could not afford an expensive funeral.

As she talked with the family, they turned to Virginia. "Can Virginia bury our baby?" they asked.

"Virginia?" replied Tillie. "Why, Virginia is not ordained, she's not a pastor. I just don't think we can do that."

"You don't understand," one of the family members said. "Virginia's the only pastor we know."

And so Virginia, less than five years a Christian, less than five years away from a helpless and hopeless lifestyle, helped the people of her community find hope by conducting a funeral service. The only training she had was living among the multihousing residents who shared her culture and life experiences. It was enough.

5.

A MULTIHOUSING STRATEGY

In 1980, the Church Extension Section, Baptist General Convention of Texas, accepted the challenge of developing an effective strategy to evangelize and congregationalize the growing multihousing population in Texas. For the next twenty years, every effort was made to reach this target group through Bible study enlistment, social ministries, recreation, and other strategies. After many years, and many different projects, a workable model was not found. Dr. Charles Lee Williamson, then mission division director, made this assignment because "an effective model must include the ways and means of churching the apartment dweller on-site."[1] He wanted to start new mission churches in and around the apartment community.

A major priority was given to this assignment. J V Thomas contacted the National Multihousing Consultant of the Southern Baptist Home Mission Board, Dr. David Beal. The Home Mission Board asked Dr. Beal to move to Texas to assist in this project. Several churches were invited to cooperate by trying different approaches to multihousing mission churches. Funds were appropriated to pay salaries, rent, and other program expenses. However, nothing produced the desired indigenous congregational model.

The breakthrough came as an unexpected blessing from God. It was not planned or financed as a multihousing strategy. Rather, it was the result of the Key Church Strategy and the Indigenous Satellite method used to start mission churches.

It has been one of God's special serendipities to provide an effective multihousing strategy through the work of two women, Tillie Burgin and Barbara Oden. They lived in two different cities and, at that time, did not know each other. The professional background of these two would not seem to qualify them to be the instruments of a major paradigm shift in how to reach the multihousing dweller.

Tillie Burgin had a background in public school administration; she left her job as personnel director of the Arlington ISD, to become minister of missions at the First Baptist Church, Arlington, Texas. First Baptist Church, Arlington, had just become a Key Church.

Barbara Oden, who had a background in multihousing administration, had just become a Home Mission Board (SBC) full-time Mission Service Corps Volunteer. She was assigned to work with the First Baptist Church, Houston, Texas. First Baptist Church had just become a Key Church. The following is the story of the first new misson churches started by each of these two women.

THE TILLIE BURGIN STORY

In 1986, Tillie Burgin had just become minister of missions for the First Baptist Church, Arlington, Texas. She approached the manager of a local apartment complex about the opportunity to conduct Bible studies in the apartment community. After a brief visit, the manager asked who would lead in the Bible study. She wanted to meet this person. Tillie was stumped for a moment, but she remembered her son, Jim, was at home studying. He was a student at Southwestern Baptist Theological Seminary in Fort Worth, Texas. Tillie told the manager that she would bring the Bible study leader for her to meet.

Tillie hurried home, had Jim dress quickly, and brought her reluctant son to meet the apartment manag-

er. Permission was granted, and Jim Burgin began the process of starting a new church in the apartment community. He knocked on doors and became acquainted with the residents by building relationships. An elderly man in the complex died, and as Jim ministered to the family, they began to come to the Bible study. A core group was formed and the Bible study grew in number.

Jim and his wife, Debbie, worked at the apartment community for two years. When they graduated from seminary, they were asked to serve Lakeside Baptist Church in Dallas as minister of missions. There was no pastor left to lead the church at the apartment complex. Bob Burgin, Jim's dad, then a high school principal, agreed to substitute. For the next seven years, he continued to substitute. During this time, he retired from the Arlington ISD and gave the time needed to develop this congregation.

The church continued to grow under Bob's leadership; however, after a change in management, the church was asked to vacate the premises. A storefront was made available on Abram Street, not far from the apartments. God blessed this move of faith! In the new location, the church was able to reach out to more families in central Arlington. People came to church. They heard God's Word. They made personal commitments to Jesus as Savior and were baptized.

The name of the church was changed to Abram Street Church; they constituted in the fall of 1996. The church averages 100 people in Bible study and worship service each Sunday. They also conduct a Bible study that meets on Wednesday evenings in the clubhouse of the apartment complex where they had first organized.

THE BARBARA ODEN STORY

Barbara Oden was an apartment manager for eight years in Houston, Texas. The multihousing industry was a very lucrative business at this time. The economy was very good. People were moving to Houston in large numbers. This was an exciting job because the property could be developed almost any way a manager desired. There were so many people moving into Houston that the waiting lists for apartments were very long. It was easy to choose good clientele and to have successful properties. Profits were good, and little had to be done in the way of advertising. Gimmicks were not needed in order to attract residents. Over the period of her eight years there, things began to change as the economy of the area worsened. At first, the multihousing communities were not affected, but before long people began to move away from Houston. Soon apartment communities were merely trading residents from community to community, depending on the specials offered, the gimmicks, advertising, and the promises that were given. It was at this time that Barabara felt a definite leading of the Lord to some type of full-time Christian service. She was working with the youth in her church. Every time an opportunity came along to work with them—unless it was on Sunday—her job would stand in the way. The responsibility to the property was too great for her to leave. Still, she wanted to leave her apartment manager's job.

Barabara heard about a Baptist organization called Mission Service Corps, an organization for volunteers in missions. She decided to attend a four-day orientation to learn more about it. She felt that she was being called to work with youth, so while she was at the orientation, Barbara looked at all the requests for youth workers and pursued each of them. Nothing seemed to work out the way she had anticipated it might. One of the requests mentioned at the orientation was for someone to work with the Union Baptist Association helping to start multihousing ministries across the city.

At the end of the orientation, Barbara came home with no assignment. She decided to go to the mission center at her church, the First Baptist Church of Houston. She helped at the center until she received an assignment from Mission Service Corps. An hour before Barbara arrived, an apartment supervisor called Harvey Kneisel, minister of missions at Houston First Baptist Church. The supervisor had heard about the many things Barbara's church was doing to make life better in multihousing communities and wondered if the church might be able to help her. Her property was little more than 50 percent filled and needed something that would help with resident retention. If the church could help provide a wholesome activities program, it would make the residents want to stay because there were no programs like it in the area. She offered a free apartment for someone to live in if he or she would serve as the activities director. She also gave an apartment in which to hold the activities.

When Barbara arrived at the Mission Center, introduced herself and told of her background as an apartment manager, Harvey told her of the telephone call. Barbara could not believe it! Again, multihousing ministry was being brought to the forefront for her. Barbara told Harvey that she did not think she would be interested in this particular opportunity, but that she was willing to help in other ways. Harvey asked if Barbara would go with him to look at the property. After visiting the property and looking the situation over, she was more convinced that this was not what she wanted to do or where she wanted to be.

Yet God had another idea! As Barbara was reading John 15:16 one evening, the verse lit up like a neon sign in her mind. "Ye have not chosen me, but I have chosen you, and ordained you, that ye should go and bring forth fruit, and *that* your fruit should remain: that whatsoever ye shall ask of the Father in my name, he may give it to you" (KJV).

God was telling Barbara that this was what he had

chosen for her, that this was what he wanted her to do. In August 1986, Barbara and her two teenage children moved into the apartment to begin their ministry there.

One week after they moved into the apartment community, they held a carnival as an opening activity. They had fun playing games, eating, singing, and laughing. A youth group that was passing through the area performed a Christian musical. That day, five people accepted Christ into their hearts. This was God's affirmation. The next week they held Backyard Bible Clubs and thirty-six children and teens accepted Christ. From there, Barbara planned a number of activities, classes, seminars, and Bible studies. She tried to find out what the residents needed, realizing that if she could provide it for them she would win the right to be heard and to share Jesus.

Within a few months, there were seventy believers on this property. Barbara had been trying to take them to church but without much response. With this many new believers, it seemed that something needed to be done to provide them with a pastor and a congregation on site. They needed fellowship, teaching, discipleship, and all of the rest that helps one grow to be a mature disciple. A young couple agreed to serve as church starters to begin a mission church on location. The attendance in the mission Bible studies and worship grew to about seventy persons. An adjacent apartment was rented, and with permission of the management, was renovated to provide for kindergarten through adult education space. This on-site mission church became a great success. A multihousing mission church gave the members of the sponsor church an opportunity to provide many needed ministries in this poverty-stricken community of school dropouts and drug users, crime and hunger. Eight young men and six young women are now in college or have completed college because of the encouragement by this mission church. All eight of the men are studying in the mission ministry; one has graduated and has an assignment with the Foreign Mission Board, SBC. The six young women are all studying with the intent of becoming missionaries. Two couples have left the church to plant Indigenous Satellite Churches in multihousing communities.[2] Stan Felder, after nearly ten years with this congregation, has moved to another state to serve as a full-time church planter.

Churches began sending their leaders to Arlington and Houston to find out how these two women were successfully starting mission churches in multihousing communities. Both women were asked to conduct training conferences telling how they were able to start effective ministries. Ministers of missions in other Key Churches began to use the same concepts to develop the mission church congregations in multihousing communities. Tim Ahlen, Stuart Perkins, Harvey Kneisel, and Jim Burgin were among the early leaders in the development of multihousing congregations. The Home Mission Board, SBC, with the help of these persons, began to develop materials and conduct training throughout the nation. It was from this beginning that a multihousing strategy was born.

Today, more than twelve years later, Tillie Burgin is still minister of missions at the First Baptist Church of Arlington, Texas. It is hard to overstate the impact of her multihousing ministry. She has designed an evangelistic church-starting strategy called *Mission Arlington*. Mission Arlington has Bible study and worship services in over two hundred apartment communities. It reaches between three and four thousand persons each week, and involves an additional two thousand volunteers.

In addition to the Bible studies, Mission Arlington provides a wide range of human services to street people, abused wives, prostitutes, persons in trouble with the law, and others. On an average day, more than five hundred families receive food, clothing, health care, shelter, or transportation from Mission Arlington. They run a day care facility for the children of homeless or abused women, medical, and dental clinics.

"People around here look at Tillie and the common reference is Mother Teresa," says Arlington's former mayor, Richard Greene.[3]

Mission Arlington has become, says journalist Joe Klein, "a perfect candidate for a central role in [Texas Governor] Bush's new welfare system," where one day the Governor believes there will be a " 'one-stop shopping center' in each community, where welfare eligibility will be determined, cash payments . . . distributed for services ranging from job placement to day care."[4]

Barbara Oden serves as church extension program strategist for the Southern Nevada Baptist Association, Las Vegas, Nevada. She moved from a volunteer to a program staff person and developed a multihousing strategy for the Union Baptist Association, Houston. She was appointed a full-time missionary by the Home Mission Board, SBC, and served for several years in the Metropolitan New York Baptist Association, working in the multihousing community.

Barbara Oden and Tillie Burgin have both conducted scores of conferences throughout the United States. Because of these two Key Church Strategists, Southern Baptists and other denominations have an effective multihousing strategy.

A Multihousing Strategy

People have worked hard to make their churches inviting places to come and worship. They cannot imagine why anyone would not want to come and worship with them. With so many empty places waiting to be filled in their own buildings, the thought of starting new churches just doesn't seem to make sense. When they look outside the stained-glass windows of their buildings, they become aware of an increasing number of apartments going up in the community. These communities are almost like small towns—fifteen hundred to two thousand people or more tucked away into the city landscape. In many places, almost half of a city's population lives in some kind of multihousing. The percentage is increasing.

Starting a church in a multihousing community is an alien idea to many of our churches. Yet, multihousing churches are a necessary and effective way to share the gospel with a group of people who are largely unchurched. In fact, starting churches in multihousing has been one of the most successful parts of the Key Church Strategy.

Often, it is the Christian who has never been to seminary who is best able to reach multihousing residents. The steps to starting this kind of church are the same as for any other new church: (1) find out the characteristics of the people who live there, (2) find out what their needs are, (3) then meet those needs in the power of the life-changing love of Jesus Christ.When a church does this, a new, worshiping congregation of believers is frequently the result.

Who Are Multihousing Residents?

Why People Live in Multihousing

Dr. Milfred Minatrea, formerly Director of Church and Community Ministries at the Dallas Baptist Association, notes that there are at least four reasons people live in multihousing communities:

1. Some live there because the government or some other agency is providing the housing for them. Section 8 communities (government housing projects), jails, and nursing homes are three different examples of this kind of multihousing. People living in these kinds of communities have very limited, if any, choice as to their place of residence. Such people may or may not be sympathetic toward traditional church culture. However, because it is difficult for them to move away from their homes, they are most easily reached "on-site."

2. Other people live in multihousing communities for economic reasons. Such people will likely live in multihousing most, if not all, of their lives. These folks have very little in common with traditional church culture and make up one group for whom on-site multihousing missions is essential.

3. A third group of multihousing residents is made up of people who are living there as a temporary means to gain other housing. Typically, young adults, who grew up in single-family homes, move into apartments in order to save money for a down payment on a house. They are likely to have come from a more traditional culture and intend, one day, to return to it. This group of people will usually assimilate very well into traditional churches.

4. A fourth group, according to Dr. Minatrea, is made up of those who live in multihousing by choice. These may be well represented by all socioeconomic levels. Of particular interest are those of upper income who live in expensive high-rises. Such people typically build their relationships where they work or play. It is sometimes very difficult to reach them with a ministry that focuses on geography (where they live).[5]

Why Multihousing Residents Are Unique People

The multihousing subculture is unique when compared with the culture in which most "church people" live. Traditional churches represent a rural culture steeped in biblical tradition, typically middle-class Americans with middle-class traditional values. Multihousing residents are different for a number of reasons.

Multihousing residents are urban. Consider the following statistics:

1. In 1950, barely half of all Americans lived in the cities.
2. In 1992, 77 percent of all Americans were urban.
3. By 2000, some project that almost 90 percent of all Americans will be city dwellers.

Of course, the dominant form of housing in the cities is multifamily housing. This means that the vast majority of multihousing dwellers live in urban areas. They think in urban terms and value urban life situations. For example, author Tim Ahlen's youngest daughter, Katy, grew up in the Dallas/Fort Worth metroplex.[6] During a family trip through rural Georgia, Katy was asked if she would like to live in one of the large antebellum mansions that are common in the region. Looking at one of the beautiful tree lined driveways leading back to one such mansion, she said, "No way! People could be hiding behind those trees waiting to mug me! I'd be scared to death!" This is from a girl who hears gunshots almost every night in her neighborhood and drives alone through the inner city of Dallas without fear!

Multihousing residents are secular. We have already mentioned that 85 to 97 percent of multihousing persons are not reached by any church of any denomination. Therefore, multihousing residents are secular people. George Hunter lists several characteristics of secular people, many of which apply to multihousing residents:

1. *They are ignorant about basic Christianity.* It is hard to believe that we live in an age where some Americans have never heard that Jesus Christ offers salvation to those who confess and believe in him; but the number of people ignorant of the Christian faith is increasing.
2. *They are seeking life before death.* Urban life brings such tremendous pressures many multihousing residents feel they do not know how to live in this life. Our first task, then, is to show people how the gospel can liberate them to live this life to the fullest. Only then will they hear what we have to say about the next life.
3. *They have a negative image of the church.* The media today almost universally portray a negative image of the church, whether through a sitcom caricature of a Christian or a real-life image of a televangelist. For one who has never associated with positive Christian role models, there is nothing to offset the negative images.
4. *They suffer multiple alienations.* People in a secular culture are alienated from almost everything: nature, friends, family, coworkers, and God. The biggest problem facing many multihousing dwellers is loneliness.

5. *They are untrusting of others.* Only a fool trusts someone he does not know. Secular culture is a culture of strangers, where every person is an island in a sea of faceless humanity. Frequently, the first task for multihousing ministers is to build trust with the people by getting to know them.

6. *They cannot find "the Door."* Although they are busy pursuing life in this world, they sense there is something missing. They know that there must be a door somewhere, but apart from Jesus Christ they cannot find it or open it.[7]

Multihousing residents are multiethnic. Traditionally, Americans tend to live, work, and play with people who share their ethnicity and socioeconomic standing. This has been especially true for Anglo-Americans, who have been the dominant ethnic group for the last two centuries. America, in general, and multihousing residents, in, specific are becoming increasingly multiethnic. The statistics listed below highlight our changing complexion:

1. In 1900, only about 13 percent of Americans belonged to ethnic minorities. By 2000, that percentage will be about 30 percent.

2. By 2056, the average American will trace his or her roots back to Africa, Asia, or the Hispanic world, not to Europe. Anglo-Americans are already a minority in cities like Dallas, Texas, where they comprise only 49 percent of the population.

3. Many ethnic minorities either choose or are forced to live in multihousing. Many Anglo-Americans are likewise making the same choices. Members of the majority and the minority alike are finding themselves much closer to "different folks" than they used to be.

Multihousing residents are becoming either working class or upper class. The backbone of American culture has traditionally been the middle class. America's dreams and values have largely been determined by this group. Middle-class culture has been predominantly suburban or rural in its orientation. Home ownership has been one of the chief goals of middle-class Americans; however, this is changing. Consider that in 1973, approximately 57 percent of

Americans could be identified as socially and economically middle class. However, by 1985, only 39 percent fell in this category.

This means an economic bipolarization is occurring. In plain terms, there are increasing numbers of both the very poor and very rich. Both groups are much more likely to live in multifamily housing than are middle-class people.

Why Multihousing Residents Do Not Attend Traditional Churches

One question that ought to come to mind is, "Why do multihousing residents not attend traditional churches?" That few of them do is now common knowledge. The one characteristic common to all multifamily residents is that over 90 percent of them are unchurched. It is not that they are uninterested in God. Rather, it is that traditional churches do not minister to their needs. Why have the churches failed to reach the multihousing residents? David Beal suggests four prominent myths that have held traditional churches back:

1. All multifamily residents are seeking privacy and are exclusive.
2. Residents do not stay long enough to become involved in a local church.
3. Multifamily residents are second-class citizens.
4. Management does not want the church ministering in the multifamily housing community.[8]

Belief in these myths leads traditional churches to conclude that multihousing residents are not reachable. This attitude is communicated to the residents, who rightly conclude they are not welcome in many traditional churches.

Another factor acting to diminish the participation of multihousing residents in traditional churches is the failure of traditional churches to meet residents where they are. Recent surveys of multihousing residents have shown that the most common answer to the question, Why do you think most people do not attend church? is that traditional programs and times do not fit their lifestyles or schedules. This response illustrates the gap between the rural culture of most mainline churches and the urban culture of multihousing residents. Rural people have no problem setting aside Sunday morning for church services and Bible study. Urban people may work on Sundays, or third shifts, or have schedules where Sunday is their only day of rest (the concept of Sunday being a day of rest is novel to many church folk!). People who live an urban lifestyle might rather give up a weeknight or Saturday evening for church rather than Sunday morning. If the church expects to influence these people for Christ, it must begin to see them with God's eyes, and to meet their needs when and where they are.

The most significant impediment to assimilating multihousing residents into traditional churches has to with their ignorance of the real Christian faith. As George Hunter points out, most people in our country are not *agnostics,* but *ignostics;*[9] that is, ignorant of the basic facts of Christianity. On the other hand, it is assumed that when one walks in the door of any church, he or she knows Christian language—what it means to be "washed in the blood"— or has a functional knowledge of the doctrinal belief system of the church. Most church members never stop to realize that even a simple sentence like "Jesus died for you" is incomprehensible until the person hearing it understands the twelve or more basic biblical doctrines that undergird it. Consequently, we have created churches that communicate a faith with a "calculus level" of sophistication, when the people who most desperately need to hear the church's message are grappling with spiritual concepts at the level of "elementary arithmetic." When multihousing agnostics (or any other agnostics) walk into a traditional church, they are likely to conclude that Christianity is not for them, or is irrelevant, simply because they do not understand what is going on!

How Do We Get Started in Multihousing Ministry?

Clarify Your Objectives

This awareness is what has led scores of churches all over the country to establish a multifamily housing ministry. This ministry begins with three overall objectives:

1. To establish a holistic ministry in individual multihousing communities to meet spiritual, physical, emotional, and social needs.
2. To lead multihousing residents to a saving faith in Jesus Christ, and to form an indigenous church within each community.
3. To employ methods that are both sustainable and reproducible by the residents themselves. Using such methods enables the ministry to continue should the sponsor church need to discontinue the ministry.

Discover What the Residents' Needs Are

The key to starting successful multihousing churches is to apply the good news of the gospel to the real and perceived needs of the residents. This takes some time and study, and it involves two steps.

1. *Meeting the Manager.* The first step is to establish cooperation with the management and ownership of individual multihousing communities. All work in multihousing communities is at the mercy of the manager, management company, and owner. From their perspective, the community is primarily a job, business, or investment. They are very protective of their property and are cautious about whether to allow any outside activities on-site. For this reason, we must appeal to them, and show them that the ministry offered can enhance the sense of community among the residents, and thereby, help to sustain or improve their occupancy rates.

After meeting with the multihousing manager, a management survey is conducted to determine statistical information about the community and identify the felt needs of the management. It is at this time that a commitment is sought from the management to allow work to begin in the community.

2. *Meeting the Residents.* Once permission has been gained to work on the property, the next step is to identify the felt needs of multihousing residents. To accomplish this, door-to-door surveys

have been done using a "resident interest survey." Resident surveys may be done any time, but in order to ensure maximum contact, a time should be selected when most residents can be expected to be home; for example, on Saturday mornings from 10:00 to 12:00. Typically, contact is made with 25 to 40 percent of the units on each survey. This is enough to get a representative sample of the residents. Follow-up surveys for residents missed on the initial survey are planned primarily as a means to further establish a relationship with the community. Specific totals for the multihousing communities are tallied from the resident interest survey in order to find out the main interests of the residents.

The survey tells the multihousing ministry team what the residents perceive their needs to be. Once the ministry team understands what the residents are concerned about, they can determine how the gospel can be applied to the felt needs.

Meeting the Needs

Meeting the needs of multihousing residents requires a strategy tailored for an individual multihousing community. This strategy begins when the survey results are brought to the multihousing manager. An appeal is made based on the residents' interest that the community provide a free two-bedroom or clubroom unit in which to conduct activities. In today's rental market, with relatively low occupancy rates, managers are frequently willing to provide the free space.

A core group of four or more workers is recruited for each ministry. A director or mission pastor will function as the leader of the ministry. His or her focus will be directed primarily toward planning for recruiting other workers. A second worker is assigned to work with adults. This worker is responsible for starting a Bible study, evangelism, counseling, and social service referrals for the adults in the community. The other core group members will work exclusively with children and youth. Ideally, the core group should be enlisted before conducting the resident survey. If this has not been possible, the core group should spend time on the property before proceeding with the strategy formulation.

Once the resident survey has been accomplished, the core group should synthesize and prioritize the felt needs. The needs felt or perceived by all three groups (residents, core group, and management) are listed. These needs are then prioritized according to those felt by all three groups.

What's Next?

The next step is to develop the ministry until it becomes a self-supporting, self-governing, and self-multiplying ministry. It takes prayer, planning, and perseverance, but it is well worth it all when you stop to realize that everyone you touch with the gospel of Jesus Christ will have his or her eternities radically changed! Always bear in mind that what you are doing is starting a church. It may not look like a church. It won't have a paid pastor, fancy building, padded pews, or a robed choir. Still, it will eventually become a community of people who believe in Jesus Christ as their Lord and Savior, study the Bible together, pray and worship together, share their faith with nonbelievers, support missions, tithe, and make their own decisions under the guidance of the Holy Spirit. Isn't that what a church is all about?

Meet Management and Ownership

One of the most obvious differences between multihousing ministry and other traditional church planting efforts is that it is an attempt to establish work on private property. The simple fact is that the success of multihousing ministry is dependent on the continued approval of the management and ownership. With this in mind, understanding both the owner and manager becomes very important. Cooperation will ensure a friendly relationship.

1. *The Owner.* Ownership of multihousing properties may be one of several forms. Some properties are owned by a single owner. Others are owned by partnerships or corporations. The kind most frequently encountered in multihousing ministry is the single, private owner who also serves as the property manager. Occasional-

ly, this person will own more than one property. When this happens, the owner usually splits his time between the properties, leaving day-to-day operations to a resident manager. When an ownership group owns a multihousing property, the local church will rarely have contact with the owners themselves. Depending on the size and the holdings of the group, the owners may employ or organize their own management company. The multihousing minister will usually deal with these people.

Regardless of the amount of contact with the owner, an understanding of what motivates him or her is important. Multihousing ownership is an investment, and profit is of primary importance. This means when a church approaches an owner about starting a Christian ministry on his property, that owner will usually make his or her decision on the basis of probable financial loss or gain.

2. *The Area Supervisor.* Area supervisors are employed either by the management company or directly by the owners. Supervisors may oversee the operation of various properties in a given area. The supervisor must keep the owner/management company satisfied. The bottom line is profit and loss. Area supervisors maintain control of expenses and make regular reports touching each individual property. In addition, they oversee collections and eviction proceedings, together with supervising and motivating the resident manager.

The supervisor regularly spends time each week on all of the properties assigned to her or him. Usually, the supervisor has authority to make decisions regarding any activities allowed on the property. Sometimes, the supervisor sets the policies; other times, the owner or management company does. In any event, the resident manager will usually have to consult the supervisor before allowing any new activities or ministry on the property.

3. *The Resident Manager.* The person with whom most contact is made is the resident manager. The resident manager has a multitude of responsibilities. The most important of these is to keep the property running smoothly. Other responsibilities include keeping

the financial ledger up to date, making regular reports to his or her supervisor, rent collection, showing and leasing apartments, initiating eviction proceedings, supervising support personnel, and maintaining a good relationship with the residents. Since the manager usually lives on the property, he or she is on the job twenty-four hours a day. This is a very stressful job with mediocre pay. Thus, the turnover rate for multihousing managers is very high.

The last thing a multihousing manager needs is more responsibility or something else to supervise. Because he or she is overworked and understaffed, the manager will have limited time to provide activities for the residents. If it is a low-income property, the manager will usually be skeptical that such activities help. On a higher-income property, managers may doubt that there will be any interest on the part of their residents. It will usually take some convincing to show the multihousing manager that the offered ministry can be a benefit without increasing the manager's workload.

4. *The Support Personnel.* The number and kinds of support personnel will vary from property to property. Included may be a leasing agent, assistant manager, secretary, and groundskeeper, and security, janitorial, and maintenance personnel. Some personnel may live on the property, others may not. These can be great resource people. The multihousing minister should seek to develop a good relationship with them. Care must be taken, however, not to distract them from their prescribed duties. Distracting them will put you at odds with the manager or owner.

Get Permission to "Hang Out" on the Property

One of the most descriptive phrases in multihousing ministry is "hanging out on the property." It is only by hanging out on the property that the core group can meet the residents. It is the way to develop relationships with them. It is the way to be accepted as a part of the community. It is the way to have a successful multihousing ministry.

"Hanging out on the property" can take place in any number of places: at the dumpster or laundry room; at the club room, pool, or the tennis courts; in the manager's office or a resident's apartment. Anywhere people can meet one another in a multihousing community is a good place to hang out.

Before hanging out on the property, two preliminary steps need to take place. Get permission from the manager to come onto the property. Then, meet the residents and find out about their interests. By showing an interest in them, you can build relationships while hanging out on the property.

Setting the First Appointment

The initial request to enter the property will usually be to the resident manager. There are several points to remember when making this contact.

1. Never drop in unannounced on the multihousing manager. Always make an appointment.
2. Avoid making contacts early in the morning or late in the day.
3. Rent collections occur around the first of the month. This means that the most stressful times for the manager are between the twenty-fifth of the month to the tenth of the following month. Try to schedule initial contacts with managers during the middle of the month.
4. Dress well when meeting the manager. Be professional, friendly, and attentive.
5. Know exactly what you are going to say ahead of time, and keep the meeting brief.

Conducting the Management Survey/Interview

During the first meeting with the manager, two goals should be accomplished: Obtain permission to come onto the property, and interview the manager to find out about his or her perceptions of the needs on the property. Several points should be made as a part of the appeal to come onto the property. These are:

1. *Start with who you are.* Introduce yourself, as well as the church or ministry organization you represent. It is important

for you to make it clear that you represent a respected, well-established church or group and are not simply out on your own.

2. *Find out who they are.* Gather the important statistical information about the complex and its residents. If possible, conduct this survey during the first meeting. Ask the manager about the makeup of the residents: their needs, problems, and interests.

3. *Explain exactly what is being offered.* Give the manager a clear, concise description of the kinds of services and activities offered. Let the manager know that the activities provided will be tailored to the unique makeup of the property's residents. To find out the residents' particular interests, ask permission to take an interest survey. Even if the manager does not usually allow door-to-door solicitation, he will usually allow the survey to be taken.

4. *Outline who benefits from the multihousing ministry.* Explain that the residents will benefit from the program of activities and social interaction provided. Next, explain that the management will benefit from the church's presence on the property. A spirit of community and improved resident satisfaction at the complex will result in better occupancy rates and less turnover (and more profit!). In addition to this, the management will benefit from someone taking the responsibility for the provision of social activities for the residents. This will make the manager's work lighter, giving him or her more time to work on the day-to-day duties of running the complex. Finally, show that the sponsoring church will benefit from the arrangement. The manager will know that some benefit from this ministry must result for anyone willing to provide it. Be honest in explaining that the church will benefit by having a place where its interested members can be involved in ministry that meets people's spiritual needs.

5. *Let the manager know that the desire is for the ministry to continue indefinitely.* It will be there to provide activities as long as the manager wants it for the property. Assure the manager that if any problems arise, you will do everything

within your power to resolve them. If at any time the management feels the arrangement is no longer desirable, they may ask the church to discontinue the ministry. Assure them that it will be done with all expediency should the need arise.

6. *Outline specifically what is being requested from the manager.* Initially, this will include permission to come onto the property and conduct an interest survey. A place to meet and publicity in the multihousing newsletter will be needed. Additional information for programming and evaluation of ongoing activities will be of importance.

7. *Provide a list of references to the manager.* Ideally, this should be a list of other properties where the church currently has established ministries. If no other ministries exist, provide a list of contact names and numbers of appropriate staff members within the church.

Meet the Residents

The Residents' Interests Survey

Once the manager grants permission to come onto the property, the next step is to meet the residents and discover what felt needs and interests they have. Whenever possible, the best approach is to use a door-to-door interest survey. Where door-to-door surveying is not possible, mail the survey out to residents. You can also leave it in the office to be picked up and returned when the residents pay rent. Another option is to hold a multihousing residents meeting where a group interview can take place. If none of these plans prove successful, it may be necessary to simply spend time on the property visiting with the residents in recreation or laundry areas. Attempting to program activities without the input of the residents simply will not work.

Set Priorities, Determine Resources

Once the residents interests are determined, it will be necessary to decide which activities to provide first. This is frequently a challenge, because the residents usually have more interests than there are workers. One way to narrow the choices is to compare the needs with the resources available to meet those needs. What are the gifts of the core group? Let each one minister according to his or her gifts and talents.

The whole church will be of great help here as well. Ask the pastor to plan a "Multifamily Ministry Calling Out Service." Using a missionary theme, the service can underscore the tremendous number of needs uncovered at the multihousing complex. The invitation can be geared toward asking the congregation for a commitment to provide human and financial resources to meet those needs. It may be surprising how many people can devote an afternoon a week or one Saturday morning a month to conduct special interest seminars or craft classes. Once resources are identified, prayer, organization, and implementation of the most feasible programs should follow. Do not try to do more than can be done with a reasonable amount of effort.

Enlist the Core Group

Once permission to begin work in the community has been gained and a completed Resident Interest Survey is in hand, the next step is to gather the core group together. By this time, it is known who is going to work in the ministry. If additional workers are still needed, there are three main avenues for recruiting them.

1. *The Church.* The place to start is with the local church. Work through the existing church leadership and structure to locate people who are willing to volunteer for ministry. Use a Multifamily Ministry Calling Out Service. Another way to locate possible workers within the church is with a volunteer survey. The benefit of a volunteer survey is that it allows leaders to see immediately where a person's gifts, talents, and interests lie.
2. *Friends.* Talk with friends, members of Sunday school classes, family members, and coworkers, and tell them of the opportunities for Christian ministry.
3. *Multihousing Residents.* One of the best places to locate

additional workers is from the multihousing community itself. Often when doing the Resident Interest Survey, you will meet some Christians living in the community. Since they are already a part of the multihousing community, they will have a special interest in seeing a successful Christian ministry in the community.

A minimum of four workers is needed to start the ministry. Two should be designated to work with children, one to organize adult activities, and one to be chaplain, director, or adult Bible study leader. There are some temptations to avoid at this point. Do not proceed until the core group has been completely assembled. Without a sufficient base of workers, the ministry will be spread too thin and become frustrated. The other temptation to avoid is to concentrate on children's work only. Children will be quick to respond to the ministry; they will respond to virtually any attention. Their response will be so great, however, that all available time can be spent working only with children, leaving no time for adults. For this reason, two of the ministry team members should concentrate their ministry toward adults.

Cultivate Relationships

Our country is filled with contradictions. We are among the wealthiest of nations, yet an increasingly large number of our people are living in poverty. The nation's scientific knowledge and technology are unsurpassed, yet the illiteracy rate is appalling. One can talk with people around the world in a matter of seconds, yet find it difficult to talk to the person next door.

It is in the midst of these contradictions that God sends people to proclaim the gospel. Sometimes, because of these contradictions, the people to whom God's great gift of salvation is sent never hear the message. As Paul says, "How can they believe in the one of whom they have not heard?" (Romans 10:14). One of the greatest challenges in evangelism is to cultivate a relationship with people so they can hear the message. Special community events are one way of developing these relationships.

Community events and activities ought to have three objectives: (1) They should facilitate personal relationship building among residents and the ministry team; (2) they should build a sense of community on the property; (3) most important, they should lead residents to take a step, however small, toward establishing a relationship with Jesus Christ.

Being Incarnational

Have you ever wondered why the heavenly Father chose to proclaim his salvation the way he did? Why did he have to send his Son Jesus Christ? Couldn't he just as easily have orchestrated a large-scale angelic choir (like the one he did for the shepherds) to go on tour through the whole world? Couldn't he have organized a heavenly leaflet drop that declared our need to "get right or roast"? He did not do that. Instead, he chose to become a human being. God became flesh and made his dwelling among us! That way he could begin to cultivate a relationship with us—a relationship that would become intimate and effective for salvation. He wanted to be "up close and personal."

When the multihousing ministry team first walks onto the property, its members' first task will be to cultivate close relationships with the residents of the community. There is no substitute for this approach to outreach. To be effective, the team must also "become flesh and make our dwelling among them."

Cultivating relationships requires an understanding of the people who live in the community. Apartment residents are not all the same. Some of the people living in any multihousing community will be new move-ins. Newcomers have many needs. Some of these needs are very ordinary. For example, new residents need to know where the laundry room and dumpsters are and where to get the best pizza.

Other needs are more significant. A new home means a new start in life. A new job is often involved. Some newcomers are searching for new relationships and friends. These people are relatively easy for members of the ministry team to get to know.

Not all newcomers are looking for relationships. Some have sufficient relationships (family and friends) living in the general vicinity of the multihousing community. Others, for one reason or another, are loners. Establishing relationships with these newcomers requires discernment and patience on the part of ministry team members.

Some of the people in the community are long-term residents. Like the newcomer, they may or may not be interested in relationships. Many "old-timers" have lived in their particular multihousing for months or years and still do not know their neighbors. They can be greatly helped if they can become part of a community.

Others know everybody and everything that happens at the property. Some of the old-timers may function as community leaders. They can become valuable helpers in organizing the community. If they can be won to Christ, they can become leaders—even pastors—of the mission congregation. One of the first tasks of the multihousing ministry team should be to identify these "gatekeepers" to the community and enlist their help in developing the new work.

Community Events and Personal Relationships

Large-scale events are not the best occasions for developing close personal relationships. Ordinarily, a quieter, more intimate setting is needed to carry on meaningful conversation. Still, community events can be helpful in at least two ways: (1) they can help break the ice with people who are not known; (2) they provide an opportunity for the residents to see a "church person" at play. Community events are among the least threatening ways a multihousing minister can become acquainted with the multihousing residents. One of the best ways to build a sense of community is to organize some community activities on the property. What forms these take will vary greatly according to the needs of residents. They may be special interest seminars, parties, or fellowships, community service, and so forth.

Planning a Community Event

The key to planning community events is to know the community. What works for one community might not work in another. Community events will be most successful if these steps are followed:

1. What needs can this event meet in the community? It is important to "scratch where it itches."
2. Get permission from the manager.
3. Determine what resources are needed.
4. Publicize the event one or two weeks in advance and again on the day of the event.
5. Include the residents in planning and conducting the event.
6. Begin and end on time.

Evangelism and Community Events

Not all community events will be overtly evangelistic. Some will be primarily to develop awareness of the ministry or to foster friendships among the residents. However, the multihousing ministry team must ensure that, in some way, every event should help the multihousing residents take one step closer to the Savior. The examples below were all activities done in multihousing ministries in Dallas and Fort Worth, Texas, through the multihousing ministries of Gambrell Street and Cliff Temple Baptist churches. Note how in each case a relationship building event also included some element of evangelistic activity

1. **Free Yard Sale.** Crossroads Chapel had a free yard sale in October. The weather had just changed with a cold snap. People were in need of sweaters, coats, and jackets. Crossroads Chapel has a clothes closet, but many of the people were embarrassed to come and get clothes. To meet this need, tables were placed in the courtyard. Some residents brought their extra clothing and placed it on the tables along with the chapel's stock. People needing clothes took items according to their need. At the end of each table were free

Bibles and tracts in English and Spanish. By the end of the yard sale, all of the Bibles and many of the tracts were taken. This was a first step in sharing the gospel with some people. Spiritual needs as well as physical needs were met.

2. **Thanksgiving Dinner.** Thirty-five residents of Crossroads Multihousing came and ate dinner at the Community Thanksgiving Meal of Gambrell Street Baptist Church on the Wednesday before Thanksgiving. Fellowship took place during the meal. The program included a short devotional time and prayer. At least two people who came to the dinner later came to Crossroads to worship.

3. **Fall Festival in Place of Halloween.** Crossroads Chapel had a party with good wholesome games and a devotional time for the children of the community. Costumes were permitted as long as they were not violent or evil in nature. Almost fifty children and adults participated in this very successful event.

4. **Movie Night.** Use a VCR and television set to hold a movie night for either children or adults. Movies can be decidedly evangelistic—for example, The Jesus Film. Another option is to show a wholesome movie that expresses Christian values. Serve popcorn and soft drinks and the people will give a good response.

5. **Block Party.** Block parties are perhaps the most successful community events a church can sponsor. Enlist some live music, serve some free food, organize some games for the kids, and it will be sure to get maximum participation from the community. Make sure some volunteers have tracts and Bibles to give away. They should also be ready to share their faith. It is common to see forty to fifty people make personal commitments to Christ out of a crowd of 200 to 300 people. More information on block parties is available from denominational sources. Toby Frost, of the North American Mission Board, SBC, has written a very useful pamphlet on block parties.[10]

6. **Book Lending Service.** Compile a library of Christian self-help books (subjects dealing with relationships, parenting, alcohol and drug abuse, spiritual questions, and so forth. Go from door to door and offer to lend them to the residents for

a specific period. By observing which selections are of interest to them, one will get to know the areas of life where they are struggling. Cultivate the relationship along the lines of helping them meet that need.

7. **Bible Studies.** Some communities will have individuals who are open to Bible study right from the beginning. The first Bible study should be for a short and definite duration (four to six weeks), and should teach the basics of the Christian faith.

8. **Special Interest Seminars.** Family finances, personal safety, basic car repair, and job search skills are all topics of special interest that help the multihousing ministry team cultivate relationships. As with the Bible studies, these seminars should last no longer than four to six weeks. In addition, they should be at a very basic level.

9. **Community Needs Ministries.** Occasionally, there will be a need for some kind of community ministry, such as afterschool care, food pantry or clothing closet, ESL, or GED classes. These can be very effective at cultivating relationships. However, careful consideration should be used before starting one of these ministries since they require long-term commitments of time and resources.

Many churches try to do multihousing ministries and fail because they never learn how to cultivate relationships with the residents of the community. They conduct seminars, Bible studies, or other events, but no one comes. If this has been experienced, try to get to know people rather than to conduct a program. Take the time required to build meaningful relationships with people, and the team will discover that the incarnate Christ will manifest through their ministry.

Develop the Mission

Core Group Development

During the mission development phase of the ministry, perhaps the most important area of work is core group development. The core group is to be made up of the multihousing ministry team, and the adults who make a commitment to the mission during the first Bible studies. These people are the future leaders of the mission.

Care should be taken to foster a sense of partnership and camaraderie between the two groups. All should be committed to the goals of the ministry. Each person, even the new Christian, needs to have a job that contributes to the mission's work. The group should have regularly scheduled times for Bible study, prayer, and fellowship.

Worship Services

Worship is a central part of the Christian experience that expresses itself in a variety of ways. In the multihousing setting, worship may take place on Sunday mornings at 11:00 or at another time that is convenient for the residents of the community. The service may be formal with a written order of worship, or it may be entirely unstructured, with church members testifying, singing, praying, or preaching as the Spirit leads.

Sunday School (Bible Study)

The establishment of a graded Sunday school may take place either at the same time worship services begin or later. The Sunday school may begin with just two or three children's classes and one adult class. If there are enough workers, students, and space, more classes may be added.

To help with the continual need of worker training, some apartment ministry organizations provide an ongoing periodic workers' meeting. Inexperienced teachers can be taught their lessons and given ideas on methods during these meetings. The sessions can be a time of encouragement and spiritual growth.

A key to successful Sunday school in the apartment setting is flexibility. If the teachers expect conditions and resources to be the same as they find in their home church, they are not going to be effective. Conditions for Sunday school are usually far from ideal when it comes to space and worker-to-student ratios. However, the following suggestions may be of some help:

1. Always have at least two children's workers for each children's class.
2. Do not hesitate to enlist apartment residents as workers in Sunday school.
3. Be prepared to enlist the apartments of residents for use as Sunday school areas.
4. If the management has provided a free apartment for meetings, then use that one for the children. Let the adults use someone's residence.
5. While the best environment for teaching is always desirable, remember that even in the worst conditions, the children will learn more than if the teacher was not there at all!

Discipleship Training

When the mission develops to the point that there are several people who are in need of advanced discipleship, it will be time to add an hour for that purpose. The materials for discipleship training can come from a variety of sources. Check with your local Christian bookstore for appropriate materials.

Prayer Meeting

No church will be what God wants it to be if its members do not spend time together in prayer. In the beginning of a multihousing mission, prayer needs will be met each time the congregation gets together. There may come a time when the needs will be so great, and the spiritual maturity of the people is such that an entire hour together in prayer will be needed. If that time does come, then it will be appropriate to schedule a prayer meeting.

Administrative/Financial Concerns

A budget should be developed as soon as possible after the new work is begun. The budget should be large enough to challenge all the members of the congregation to give, but not so large that they will never attain the goals of the budget. Several line items need inclusion in the initial budget, usually expressed in percentages:

1. The budget should contain appropriate amounts for missions right at the start.
2. An agreed upon amount should be designated for benevolence.
3. A certain amount needs to be put aside for literature, events, and other programs of the new congregation.
4. Salaries are usually inappropriate for pastor or staff. However, some money should probably be set aside to cover expenses incurred by the pastor or other workers.

The mission should have its own checking account as soon as is practical. Avoid depositing the money with the sponsor church whenever possible, because this kind of action fosters a sense of dependency that is not healthy.

Administration of the mission church is very important. The new church needs to know which actions are permissible and which are not. They need to have doctrinal guidelines as well. To help the mission church in this regard, the sponsor church should have a policy and procedure manual to guide the new work.

Conclusion

When is the job of a multihousing ministry team done? Only when the congregation has grown enough numerically and spiritually that they do not need help from a sponsor church anymore. Typically, this milepost takes three to five years to achieve. To reach it will require more than just time. It will take hard work, a willingness to go into battle against Satan, and the kind of Christlike patience, compassion, and commitment that is willing to do whatever it takes to reach a multihousing community for Christ.

In the late 1700s, Robert Raikes, a young journalist living in Gloucester, England, looked out on the streets of his city and saw the distressing reality of a society lacking Christ. The Industrial Revolution was in full swing. Men, women, and children all worked six days a week. On Sundays, parents collapsed for a day of rest, but the children roamed the streets, unsupervised, frequently forming gangs and causing mayhem in the city.

The journalist wondered if there was anything he could do to help teach these children how to read and write, and how to know God. His solution was to begin schools for the children in which he would teach them the basic educational skills and Bible reading. Because their only day off was Sunday, he had to use the Lord's Day as a day of teaching.

The local churches were aghast. Preachers called this activity an abomination, a desecration of the Sabbath. They decried the fact that laymen were teaching the Bible. Nonetheless, the idea caught on. Soon there were schools like this popping up all over Britain. They became popular on the European continent as well. Finally, by the turn of the ninteenth century, they began to take America by storm. The movement became known as the Sunday School Movement, a phenomenon so successful at introducing people to the Christian faith that one can hardly imagine a church in America today not having one.

In America today, the challenge is as great as the one that was facing Robert Raikes. All across our land are people in need of a layperson like Robert Raikes to leave the sanctuary of the church building and take the gospel to the millions of unchurched people who live in multihousing.

APPENDIX 1
OPERATIONAL GUIDELINES

The Work of the Key Church Council

One of the most important factors that determine the long-term success of a church's Key Church program is the involvement of the church leadership in the organization and implementation of the new work. From a local church perspective, a group known as a Key Church Council provides this kind of oversight.

The Key Church Council is designed to carry out five tasks:

1. Call the people of God to pray for the local missions effort.
2. Organize the church for effectiveness and efficiency in ministry.
3. Discover unmet missions needs in the community.
4. Determine strategies to meet the needs.
5. Develop missions ministry teams to carry out the work.

A. Organization

Missions work, like any church-related activity, is often dependent upon organization or structure. Poor organization can be cumbersome. It inhibits ministry because too much energy is expended to maintain the structure. A good organization runs smoothly. It promotes ministry and focuses energy on ministry tasks. A good Key Church Council facilitates the church's local mission ministry.

The number of Key Church Council leaders depends on the size of the Key Church. A small church may begin a Key Church Council with one person interested in doing missions; larger churches would need several leaders.

Once the appropriate size is determined, the tasks of Key Church Council personnel should be well defined. Regardless of the number of persons serving, each elected leader should have a definite job, understand exactly what the job is, and know how to do it. Listed below is a sample organizational structure that works well in Baptist and other free church settings. You may need to make some modifications to it in order for the Key Church Council to fit in with your denominational practice and polity.

B. Officers

The Key Church Council should have a sufficient number of leaders to carry out mission projects. The most effective organization will include most of the following officers to share responsibilities.

1. The Key Church Council Director is the general leader who sees that each missions task is performed. The director coordinates missions through the Key Church Council and represents missions programs to the church council or the administrative board.

2. The Missions Survey Director leads the council to discover unmet needs and opportunities. The missions survey director reports to the Key Church Council. The council recommends strategies to meet the needs. The Missions Survey Director's work is not limited to a one-time survey but is a continuing discovery and assessment of needs.

3. Representatives from the Missions Auxiliary and other missions programs should participate fully on the Key Church Council. Representatives are selected by their respective programs to serve as Key Church Council leaders. They are important as liaison members. These officers are to coordi-

nate all mission plans and opportunities between the Key Church Council and their own organization.

The intention is to avoid duplicating mission activities or neglecting missions needs. Review the above list to determine what officers your church will need.

When it is discovered that missions needs are not being met, or cannot be met, by some other church organization, the Key Church Council should design strategies to meet those needs. Usually a director for each type of need is appropriate. Leaders may be needed in areas such as community ministries, ethnic ministries, new congregations, interracial ministries, chaplaincy ministries, witness to other religious groups, resort/leisure ministries, volunteerism, multifamily housing, transitional community concern, or other areas of opportunity. Election of these leaders depends on needs discovered. To increase congregational awareness, churches may want to elect some leaders before completing the needs survey.

C. Relationships

The Key Church Council maintains relationships so that neither individuals nor groups are hampered in missions performance. Good lines of communication should be established so that church supervision and support can be given to all group and individual missions activities.

1. Missions Organizations of the Church—As indicated earlier, the Auxiliary Missions representatives should serve on the Key Church Council. If these organizations do not exist in the church, the Key Church Council should see that they are established. These representatives should serve as liaisons between represented Auxiliary and Key Church Council, attempting to establish and maintain confidence and cooperation.

2. Church Council—The director of the Key Church Council should be a member of the church council/administrative

board. The director needs to have input into the calendar and budget planning process. Community needs should be shared with the council.

3. Pastor and Other Church Staff—The pastor and other church staff members should be kept informed of Key Church Council work. They should feel free to attend meetings and share insights, suggestions, and concerns.

Some Suggested Procedures and Policies for Sponsored Churches

A very helpful tool to assist the minister of missions in administration of the missions program is a document that details policies and procedures. The sample below, written for a Baptist church, may be used as a template to be edited to conform to the special requirements, doctrinal positions, and polity of individual churches or denominations.

DEFINITION

A mission church is an indigenous congregation that meets in an apartment, a storefront, a house, or other type of facility. It is a congregation that is culturally and linguistically in harmony with the people surrounding it, and finds within itself the potential to govern, support, and reproduce itself. It may continue as a permanent part of the sponsoring church's evangelism, outreach, and Bible study program (as an Indigenous Satellite Church), or it may become autonomous.

PURPOSE

The purpose of each mission church is to reach people for Christ in their local context. Principal methods will be New Testament evangelism, Bible teaching, and the discipleship of believers for Christian service.

FUNCTION

A Key Church's mission churches may vary in their ministry functions:

1. Some missions may reach lost and unchurched people and lead them into a traditional church.
2. Some missions may become long-term church satellites of the Key Church, which produces other satellite churches.
3. Some missions may develop into traditional churches.

Decisions regarding such developments will be made in accordance with the individual church's or denominational polity.

RELATIONSHIPS

1. Definition of the mission church[1]—The mission church is a fellowship of baptized believers in Jesus Christ who desire membership in the sponsoring church through the mission church. They desire the discipline of the sponsoring church and a harmonious relationship with the sponsoring church.
2. Lines of authority—The sponsor church, the mission church, and the local, state, and national judicatories will work together cooperatively to develop the new congregation.
3. Relationship to sponsor—The mission church ministry is an outreach and discipling ministry of the sponsoring Key Church. Each church is to adopt and to be in harmony with the philosophy and procedures of the sponsoring Key Church.

DOCTRINE

1. The Bible is the primary and final authority in all matters of faith and practice.

2. The Confession of Faith of the Sponsor Church or Denomination shall be the accepted position on the basic church doctrine.[2]
3. The ordinances and sacraments will be administered in accordance with the practice of the sponsoring church.

MEMBERSHIP

1. A member of a mission church shall be a member of the sponsoring Key Church with voting privileges limited to the mission congregation until her or she presents himself or herself for membership to a larger body of the sponsoring Key Church. The sponsoring Key Church shall keep mission church membership in a separate section of its records. Mission congregations will maintain records of their membership. Membership cards are available from the minister of missions when needed.
2. Persons seeking membership in a mission congregation shall be welcomed, conferred with, and presented for fellowship in the mission congregation, in accordance with the practices of the sponsoring church.
3. Members will be received as follows:
   • By baptism upon their public profession of faith in Jesus Christ as personal Savior and Lord.
   • By transfer of membership from another church of like faith and order.
   • By statement of previously professed faith in Jesus Christ, baptism, and membership in a church of like faith and order when a letter from the church in which membership was last held is not available.
   • By following membership procedures or catechism required by the sponsoring Key Church's denomination.

(Key Church Council members who join a mission congregation shall resign their position to prevent a conflict of interest.)

LEADERSHIP

1. The mission church pastor will serve as a leader of the mission congregation. No pastor may be selected without the full cooperation of the minister of missions, and confirmation by the Key Church Council and other ministries of the church as necessary.
2. In a new work situation, a pastor is chosen before a congregation has been formed. When this is the case, the minister of missions will present a recommendation by the missions committee for screening and final approval.
3. Should the pastorless congregation already be established, as in a developing or "older" work, the mission congregation should select a pulpit committee. The minister of missions will serve as an ex officio member of the pulpit committee and shall be expected to work closely with the committee. The committee's recommendation for a call should be presented to the mission committee for screening, followed by the approval of this group. The approved recommendation will then be presented to the mission congregation in an adequately publicized business session.[3]

MISSION CHURCH OFFICERS

1. The mission pastor shall serve as moderator of the congregation.
2. The vice moderator shall be a lay leader elected by the congregation.
3. A clerk and treasurer shall be elected by the mission congregation to maintain bookkeeping and financial records for the congregation.
4. The congregation shall also elect a Sunday school director and worship leader, when appropriate.
5. The congregation shall elect other leaders of program organizations and committees.

ALL LEADERSHIP

1. Leadership of the Key Church's mission churches will meet once monthly with the minister of missions.
2. New leadership for the mission ministry will complete training session led by the minister of missions and/or other qualified individuals.
3. Evangelism Explosion, or other approved evangelistic training, is required for each pastor.

ORDINANCES/SACRAMENTS

1. The mission church and its pastor have the authority to administer the ordinances and sacraments of the New Testament church, in accordance with the practices of the denomination or tradition of the sponsoring Key Church.

FINANCES

1. Each mission church will endeavor to be financially self-supporting.
2. Once a core group is established and before cultivation of the neighborhood begins, tithes and offerings should be pooled and a separate checking account opened in the name of the new congregation.
3. It is requested that two signatures be present on all checks signed.
4. A financial report is requested by the Key Church Council at the end of each month. This report will be turned into the minister of missions' office.
5. A monthly financial report will be submitted to the mission congregation at the time of the regular monthly business meeting.
6. Budget planning should be an annual procedure in each mission congregation and shared with Key Church Council. Each congregation will be asked to participate in giving financially to denominational

causes. They will also participate in the ongoing mission program of the sponsoring Key Church by contributing a minimum of 10 percent of the new church's undesignated income each month to a special fund for new mission work. This practice of mission giving will begin as the new congregation begins public worship services.

7. Attainable goals for each mission congregation will be established annually for the funding of new missions.
8. In case of a church discontinuing its ministry in an area, all funds in the checking account will revert to the sponsoring Key Church's "Church Starting Fund."
9. Any checking account of a mission church will be closed only by the Key Church's financial secretary.

BUSINESS MEETING

1. Each congregation shall hold regular monthly business meetings on a date determined by the congregation.
2. Special business meetings may be called if notice of such a meeting has been given to the congregation at Sunday worship services in advance.

MULTIPLICATION

Each new mission church will be expected to start other new churches at the appropriate time. The minister of missions will work with the new church pastor and the Key Church Council to facilitate the starting of new congregations.

APPENDIX 2
CASE STUDIES

C hurch growth has been defined in this book as evangelism—effective evangelism that results in making disciples for Jesus Christ. The effectiveness of an evangelistic strategy is gauged by the number of persons accepting Jesus Christ as Lord and Savior and being assimilated into the life and work of the local church.

The most effective form of evangelism is church starting. The discipleship process accelerates when new churches are planted. This appendix illustrates church growth by presenting case studies of several Key Churches.

The minister of missions of each church declared with humility that God had allowed him or her to accomplish more in the work of the church with the Key Church Strategy than with any other strategy he or she had ever used. With stories like these, it is no surprise that churches that have become Key Churches are starting 33 to 40 percent of the new churches across the Southern Baptist Convention.

Mobberly Baptist Church
Longview, Texas

History

In the fall of 1938, the Great Depression neared an end, and the threat of another world war did not yet cloud the horizon. A handful of believers, seeking to do the will of God, sensed the time was right for a new beginning, and so they began a new church. On Sunday, September 4, the moderator and eighty members of the South Highland Mission, sponsored by the First Baptist Church of Longview, voted to form the Southside Baptist Church.

In 1942, after four years of growth, the church purchased the property located at Mobberly Avenue and Owens Streets. They moved their building and changed the name of the church to Mobberly Avenue Baptist Church.

As the Second World War ended, the church completed the first sanctuary. They added an educational building in 1952. The second sanctuary was completed in 1957. At the opening of the summer of 1964, Mobberly's seven original Sunday school classes had grown to 36 departments, and the 80 charter members to 1,882. The Lord continued to add to the church membership.

In January 1970, our present pastor, Dr. Laney Johnson, came to Mobberly Avenue Baptist Church. Under his guidance, the church continued to grow. The church realized that if it was to continue to grow and to reach people, fulfilling the Great Commission, it must establish a satellite location in the northern part of the city. This became a reality in October 1980, when the church observed the ground-breaking ceremonies for the new location at 625 E. Loop 281. On March 6, 1981, the name of the church officially changed from Mobberly Avenue Baptist Church to Mobberly Baptist Church and became "one church family meeting in two locations."

From 1978 to 1979, the church began two ethnic missions: a Vietnamese and a Hispanic mission. These two efforts are still under the umbrella of Mobberly Baptist Church.

In October 1991, work began on expansion of the Mobberly Baptist Church facilities. The church moved into these facilities in July 1993. Mobberly Baptist Church launched a new era in its history in September 1992, when the church's two congregations reunited. On Easter Sunday, 1994, the church began another southside mission known as the Green Street Mission. This mission seeks to reach into a segment of the community that is not likely to feel comfortable attending services at the home church.

Under the leadership of Dr. Laney Johnson, who celebrated his twenty-fifth anniversary as pastor of the church in 1995, the church's membership has grown to over four thousand. This growth has called for the creation of two worship services and three Bible study hours on Sunday morning.

Present Ministry

Today, Mobberly Baptist Church's mission work is comprised of one church-type mission, three Indigenous Satellite Churches, and twelve ongoing ministries. Pastor Johnson states, "The Key Church Strategy has opened the eyes of the staff. It is beginning to open the eyes of many members to the tremendous potential for reaching out into the community and beyond to reach previously unreached people groups with the gospel of Jesus. The strategy has given us direction to begin to mobilize the members to hands-on ministry outside the walls of the church building." Pastor Johnson's vision is "to build a base of 2,000 average attendance in Sunday school. We will then plant at least thirty indigenous mission churches in the East Texas area by mobilizing the members of Mobberly to go and serve as seed members and church planters."

According to Pastor Johnson, the most effective ministries for the church have been

1. Divorce Recovery Workshops
2. Super Mom Support Group for Mothers of Preschoolers
3. First Place Weight Loss and Management Seminar
4. Village South Apartment Ministry
5. Green Street Mission
6. Prison Ministry and Nursing Home Ministry

First Baptist Church
Dallas, Texas

History

From the inception of the First Baptist Church of Dallas, there has been a strong and growing interest in missions. The very beginnings of this great church are a chronicle of missions in action. When Mr. and Mrs. W. L. Williams came to Dallas on November 17, 1867, there was no Baptist church. The Williamses, both of whom were Baptist, set about immediately to establish a Baptist church in the small but growing community. Mrs. Williams (Lucinda) tells that when she asked her landlady where the Baptist church was located, the landlady replied, "There is not one now, and I hope there will never be one." Mrs. Williams quickly told her that she was a Baptist and that there would be a Baptist church in Dallas. In the spring of 1868, Mr. Williams contacted the Reverend W. "Spurgeon" Harris and invited him to come to Dallas and hold a Protracted Meeting. Harris agreed, came in July of 1868, and held a two-week meeting. The Baptists of Dallas came together for this revival and stayed together to build a church. The Reverend Harris was a missionary who saw the need for a church in this frontier town. In August of 1886, Reverend Harris became the first pastor of the newly formed First Baptist Church of Dallas. Born out of a mission spirit, the church never lost its vision for reaching out to those who are unchurched.

As the new church grew, so did a sense of mission responsibility. As early as 1873, the new church was reaching out to the growing frontier town to share the gospel. In 1873, a Sunday school was formed at the corner of Live Oak and Cantegral streets. The church's records state that the mission Sunday school began "for the benefit of children out in that part of the city who had no Sunday school influence in their lives." This mission later moved to East Dallas to become the Gaston Avenue Baptist Church. This pattern repeated many times in the early years of the First Baptist Church. Many mission Sunday schools eventually became strong evangelistic churches. Some of these are the: Ervay Street Baptist Church, McKinney Avenue (now the Highland Park) Baptist Church, Central Baptist Church, Oak Cliff Baptist, Ross Avenue Baptist Church, Crowder Street Baptist Church, Forest Avenue Baptist Church, and Caroline Street Baptist Church.

In 1873, Pastor Weaver had an assistant pastor who had, among his many responsibilities, the responsibility of caring for these missions. By 1878, there was a permanent staff position with the title "City Missionary." The women of the church were keenly concerned for the local mission work. They led the church to employ some "Bible Women" to visit among the unchurched, report cases of material needs, and oversee mission Sunday schools. The first female city missionary was Miss Hollie Harper. She came to the church in 1894. Miss Harper visited among the various missions, working especially with women and children. A typical report for one month of her work included 165 visits, thirty-five Bibles given away, attending thirteen children's meetings involving over five hundred children, and distributing hundreds of gospel tracts. Since Miss Hollie had no transportation, ladies of the Industrial Society vied with one another to drive her in their personal carriages.

An interesting aside is the story of a German pastor who came to Dallas to establish a German-speaking church among the more than six thousand German-speaking people in a farm community just outside of Dallas. The area referred to is now known as the Live Oak/Swiss Avenue area. The Reverend Dahlkie came to the Dallas area in 1896. He visited with the leadership of the First Baptist Church to share his vision. The people of the church were eager to help him. They gave the Reverend Dahlkie a small stipend and took frequent offerings to assist him. In the beginning, there were only eighteen members. The church continued to meet on Carroll Avenue between Live Oak and Swiss Avenue until the 1970s. A beautiful building was built on the site in 1914. In 1980, the First Baptist Church of Dallas bought that same building from the Dallas Baptist Association for $30,000 and started the El Buen Pastor (The Good Shepherd) Baptist Church. This church proclaims the gospel to the more than 60,000 Spanish-speaking people in the East Dallas area today.

When Dr. George W. Truett became the pastor of FBC in 1897, the church was sponsoring three missions. By 1907, the church records show that there were four missions. As the years have come and gone, many of the missions have become autonomous churches and some have disappeared from sight. However, all of these Sunday schools and churches have given witness of the saving power of Jesus Christ.[1]

Present Ministry

With the coming of Dr. W. A. Criswell to be the pastor of the First Baptist Church, the church entered the modern era of missions. The first of these missions was the West Dallas Hispanic Mission. Soon, others followed. In 1980, there were fourteen missions associated with the First Baptist Church. The church now has thirty-one mission ministries in the Dallas area. The work includes new church starts, prisons, and juvenile detention ministries, along with ministries to the poor and homeless. They are now doing work in ten different languages. During the years since 1945, many of the missions of First Baptist Church have become autonomous churches. Since 1980, an increased number of missions have become autonomous churches.

Lakeside Baptist Church
Dallas, Texas

History

In the spring of 1936, a mission Sunday school met under some shade trees on a vacant lot on Groveland Street. Benches and songbooks were borrowed, and seven people full of faith gathered together. So they could have lights for night services, they built a platform, hung lights, and connected an extension cord to a neighbor's house. In thirty days, the attendance grew from seven to fifty. After the summer, with services held under trees, cold weather came and the group met in a home.

Growth demanded change. A vacant house, donated by some generous persons, became the new home. That Sunday, in November 1936, the people gathered and constituted into Lakeside Baptist Church.

In called conference, December 1936, the church voted to have Wednesday evening prayer meetings and accepted plans for the first church building. In February 1937, Lakeside Baptist Church dedicated the first building. Seventy-five people attended that meeting, and in June 1937, Lakeside officially associated itself with the Southern Baptist Convention.

Times were not easy for the newly formed Lakeside Baptist

Church; many occasions found the Sunday collections insufficient to pay the bills. Only determination, hard work, sweat, tears, and a trust in God kept the church going and growing.

From the beginning, Lakeside Baptist Church was mission-minded. With collections only forty dollars per month, the church voted to give 10 percent to missions.

It was in 1948 that the first services of Lakeside were held at the new Garland Road location. The laying of the cornerstone for the present-day sanctuary took place on Sunday, March 10, 1963.

Present Ministry

Lakeside has sponsored, started, and cosponsored many missions. Lakeside's current involvement in missions includes:

1. Missions: 4 Anglo middle-class; 1 Generation-X; 2 Korean; 1 Eritrean; 1 multiethnic; 2 Ethiopian; 2 Hispanic; and 1 Vietnamese. These missions have an average attendance of 1,021 each week; they reported 119 professions of faith and 58 baptisms in 1998.
2. Four apartment ministries bring the gospel to 131 attendees and report many conversions.
3. Nursing homes involve 6 volunteers from the church congregation.
4. Local ministries involve at least 225 members of the church in meeting people's needs.

Centro Familiar Cristiano Buenas Nuevas (Good News Christian Family Center) Santa Ana, California

History

In 1986, a small group of people, who were invited from the community, met to start a new church in the city of Santa Ana, California. With no money, but with a great missionary vision, the church began with a strategy to reach the unchurched Hispanic people with the gospel.

The new church was named Good News Christian Family Center. It has followed the policy and purpose of the Saddleback Valley Community Church; taking the ministry of Bible teaching, orientation, and spiritual counseling services to Hispanic families in Orange County, California.

The main campus of the church in Santa Ana has reached a regular attendance of three hundred and fifty people on Sunday mornings. The church has established a seminary called the Saddleback Hispanic Theological Center in order to equip pastors and leaders for the central church and missions. This seminary is an accredited extension of the Golden Gate Baptist Theological Seminary. Sixteen persons graduated this past year and are the pastors of missions. Many new churches are being planted throughout Orange County Baptist Association by the center's graduates who have had nine months of academic study and hands-on training. During these months, students spend five hours a day in classroom instruction and another six hours daily in the ministry areas where new churches are being started.

Present Ministry

The Good News Christian Family Center has eighteen congregations and fifty ministries. They baptize one convert for every four members in Sunday school.

Kirby Woods Baptist Church
Memphis, Tennessee

History

Kirby Woods Baptist Church began as a mission in 1980 as the result of the efforts of a group of Christian businessmen who had a deep desire to start a special kind of church in East Memphis. Kirby Woods Baptist became the first "Key Church" in Memphis, Tennessee, in 1994. The founders of the church had a vision of a church that would have a significant involvement in evangelism and missions. It would reach out with the gospel of Jesus Christ to the local community's people. It would teach and preach the

Bible as the inerrant Word of God. In addition, it would be a church that discipled its members to become effective participants as "Great Commission" Christians. They perceived the church, involved in God's will, a launching pad for other new churches. The desire was for Kirby Woods to start at least one new church every year. Southwoods Baptist Church of Memphis became the fruit of the mission vision of Kirby Woods.

Present Ministry

Kirby Woods church now sponsors four new churches in Memphis, Tennessee, as well as partnership missions with Baptist Associations in five states: New York, Michigan, Ohio, Florida, and Washington. They are also responsible for eleven community ministries.

Iglesia Bautista Resurreccion
Miami, Florida

History

Iglesia Bautista Resurreccion, The Resurrection Spanish Baptist Church, began as a department of Coral Baptist Church in Miami on March 18, 1962, under the pastoral care of Domingo Fernandez. On October 4, 1970, the church was constituted with 85 founding members.

In 1986, the church called Augusto Valverde, from Bahia Blanca, Argentina, as its new pastor. The same missionary spirit which helped this new pastoral family leave their native country would later become evident in Valverde's leading the church to experience the joy of being actively involved in missions outreach through church planting and mission congregations.

In 1991, the church had its first chance to sponsor a mission congregation of Brazilians who met in the church facilities and continued to grow. The next step was to plant a church in the fast growing Kendall area west of Miami. New Hope Baptist Mission, the fastest growing of all the missions, called its founding pastor, Deris Coto, to full-time service.

After these two experiences with sponsoring missions, the church understood the Lord was placing a special emphasis here, and began to pray that God would lead them to have a missionary zeal for this city and beyond. They already knew the joys and pains involved in mission work and were wholeheartedly committed to continue as the Lord would lead. God's immediate confirmation was another new mission. Soon thereafter, the Key Church challenge was launched; the church committed to it prayerfully and enthusiastically.

One of the pivotal things that occurred through the Key Church Strategy was the forming of a missions council. This group began to dream, pray, and plan. Their vision included not only missions congregations, but also missions outreach to the community through new ministries. As they prayed and saw the opportunities, God began to lay a burden on their hearts and on the hearts of other church members. Consequently, various new ministries were begun. Among these are an adult reading/writing program; special food and clothing distributions through block parties; and participation in a homeless ministry through a local rescue mission. The church already has a food pantry, clothing closet, jail chaplaincy, and a counseling ministry.

Present Ministry

The pastoral vision through 2001 was launched. It includes sponsoring a total of 25 missions congregations with many of these constituting during that time. This plan doubles the present missions ministry. It involves 600 members in missions opportunities through the missions congregations, short-term mission projects, and ministry opportunities.

Iglesia Bautista Resurreccion now has 6 congregations, 5 new ministries, and a baptism to attendance ratio of 1 to 12.

Celebration Church
Metairie, Louisiana

History

Celebration Church started when a small group of Christians began meeting together in December of 1988, with a vision to start a new church that would be uniquely designed to reach and minister to the people of New Orleans. The group first met in homes, then they moved to the campus of John Curtis Christian School. In September of 1989, a church was officially formed, and the Reverend Dennis Watson was called to be the first pastor.

From a first Sunday attendance of 86 people, the church has grown to over 1300. Sunday morning attendance at the end of the first quarter of 1996 was 929, not including attendance figures of 250 at the mission churches sponsored by Celebration Church. In addition to these figures, approximately 100 people attend a special Saturday night singles' service. Over the past six years, Celebration Church has been lauded as the fastest growing church in Louisiana.

Celebration Church has had to purchase new building property because the current plant cannot sustain the church's growth.

Present Ministry

Celebration Church now has five mission congregations, a detention ministry, and a Baptism-to-attendance ratio of 1 to 6.

Celebration Church also has 25 ISC's called JOY Groups, each with a leader and a mission to reach the community where the group is planted. Their philosophy statement reads:

"JOY Groups are small groups sometimes called cell groups or house churches. JOY Groups provide the structure and the context through which the church accomplishes its purposes of worship, discipleship, and evangelism. These Groups are an instrument God is using to accomplish the purposes of Celebration Church."

The Groups are a part of Celebration Church's plan to spread the Gospel around the world starting in New Orleans.

Clarkston Baptist Church
Clarkston, Georgia

History

In the fall of 1990, the Clarkston Baptist Church began an intense evaluation of its community. The church is located in a rapidly changing community made up of 65 percent multihousing. The demographics of the area indicated a tremendous amount of ethnic diversity. Though the church had been in a period of decline for about fifteen years, it had stabilized and had begun to grow again under the leadership of a pastor. What was obvious however, was that the church was no longer influencing its community.

Through church and community research, it was found that the church's style of ministry would, at best, result in reaching 25 percent of the people living in the church's field. Furthermore, that 25 percent grouping of people would be shrinking during the next ten years. Three choices were considered: (1) relocate, (2) do nothing, or (3) aggressively reach those whom God had placed in the church's Jerusalem.

The decision for the long-range planning group became obvious. During the year of research, the Lord had led the church to start two non-English-speaking language congregations and an apartment ministry. The church adopted the slogan to be "A People On Mission."

The churchs vision of ministry was to identify, evangelize, and congregationalize every unchurched group of people the Lord placed in its sphere of influence. It accepted the challenge to become Georgia's first Key Church.

Present Ministry

In the fall of 1992, the church called a minister of missions and evangelism. Since that time the church has started language ministries to the Filipino, Vietnamese, Ethiopian, and Persian communities; four apartment missions; and one retirement home ministry. Additional 1993 plans included an African American mission and six more apartment missions.

Kingshighway Baptist Church
St. Louis, Missouri

History

Kingshighway Baptist began in 1908 as a Sunday school program of St. Louis Park Baptist Church to minister to the German children of south St. Louis. The work grew and organized into the Kingshighway Baptist Church in 1914. The church purchased land and built a facility at its present location in 1920.

The first real effort at missions was in 1983 when several Southern Baptist churches in south St. Louis formed a food distribution center at Kingshighway. This became so successful that two other benevolent ministries grew out of it.

In 1991, the church adopted a Vietnamese congregation—the first mission attempt in the history of the church. Later that year, the church began a storefront mission—an Anglo chapel—to minister to a neglected area in south St. Louis.

Shortly after opening the storefront chapel, a Hispanic pastor asked and received permission to use Kingshighway's building to conduct services to the Spanish-speaking people in the area. In August of 1993, the church began a ministry to an African American community a short distance away. Then work began among the Laotians. Recently, their group requested that we assimilate them into our church program.

Present Ministry

In 1994, Kingshighway became a Key Church and called a mission director. With the members growing increasingly involved in reaching people, a contemporary worship service was begun. In 1995, the Mid-City Chapel began the Gibson Avenue Chapel for African Americans. The church's goal is to constitute at least one mission into a church each year.

The church has eight chapels with five meeting in the church building and three in rented storefront buildings in various areas of south St. Louis. The eight chapels average over one hundred in attendance each Sunday. The Kingshighway Baptist Church now averages fifty-five in Sunday school and ninety in worship services. With the exception of the pastor of the church and the Hispanic pastor, all of the workers in the church and chapels are bivocational.

The church has met with workers from two other churches in the St. Louis Metro Baptist Association to begin work among American Indians.

Conclusion

These are just a few of the many examples of churches that have adopted the One Church/Many Congregations model of church growth. As the strategy has grown from a large church program in Texas to a national strategy involving churches of all sizes and different denominations, one thing has been observed to be universally true—this strategy will revolutionize the local church and its surrounding community.

One of the Key Churches that has been referred to throughout this book is First Baptist Church, Arlington, Texas. One of the first in Texas to develop the Key Church Strategy, it is also in many ways the most successful.

About the Key Church Strategy, Tillie Burgin, the minister of missions said, "The Key Church Program has provided an excellent opportunity for more church members to become involved in ministry. There are many people, with servants' hearts, who are looking for a place to serve the Lord in their community. In addition, many mission ministries have been strengthened because people have faithfully prayed for lives to be changed and people to come to know the Lord. As a result, there has been growth in the main church as members have responded to the increased opportunities to serve the Lord in various areas of mission outreach."

The church's pastor, Dr. Charles Wade, echoes these remarks when he says, "Mission Arlington could never have begun if it had not been for the Key Church Strategy. It helps congregations call ministers of missions . . . so the church can get on with its task to reach people for Christ in our community. When we started, we already had some local missions, but they were not supervised very well because we did not have a minister to do that particular task. Our strategy at the beginning was to do a better job of encouraging the missions we already had. There were four of them. Second, we wanted to start at least six new mission outreach points. Within a year we had twenty-five; the rest has been a story of growth and outreach all across our community. Now there are over two hundred mission points where we are trying to help the gospel become active in people's lives. Two of our mission points have become full, constituted churches, and several more, we hope, will someday become full churches standing alone."

As mainstream America continues to hurtle down a postmodern path, Christianity is in danger of becoming irrelevant in the minds of most of our citizens. The church is becoming increasingly isolated, institutional, and culturally removed from the mass of unchurched people. Most secular people today do not have the slightest understanding about the meaning of the Christian faith. We think we are communicating when we share our faith, but it is like asking in English for a glass of water when our Mexican waiter speaks only Spanish. The response of our traditional churches is merely to **TALK A LITTLE LOUDER,** as if shouting will make these secular people understand. The result in our postmodern, existentially informed world, is that society smiles at us for being so quaint. Moreover, if Christianity has meaning for *us*, that's wonderful. Just don't expect *them* to come into our churches.

In a pluralistic, multicultural society in which we are all hyphenated Americans, there are two choices. The first choice is to raise our volume and hope the world finally takes notice and starts to come to our existing churches. The other choice is to intentionally begin new congregations for every lifestyle, language, and cultural group we find in our communities. If we dare, we will experience the same evangelistic explosion that so many Key Churches have already had by becoming one church with many congregations.

NOTES

1. Foundations

1. Gambrell Street Baptist Church pioneered the Key Church Strategy as a special project of the Church Extension Department of the Baptist General Convention of Texas. J V Thomas was the director of the project. The term "Key Church" began to be used in 1983 as a part of a promotional strategy to start 2,000 new churches between 1985 and 1990.

2. Ahlen was preceded as Minister of Missions by Winford Oakes, Gary Rhoades, Terri Willis, and Mike Barnett.

3. See J V Thomas's book *Investing in Eternity: The Indigenous Satellite Church Strategy* (Dallas, 1991).

4. See F. F. Bruce, *Paul: Apostle of the Heart Set Free* (Grand Rapids: Wm. B. Eerdmans, 1977), 64.

5. See I. Howard Marshall, *The Acts of the Apostles: An Introduction and Commentary* (Grand Rapids: Wm. B. Eerdmans, 1983), 125.

6. Ibid.

7. Ibid.

8. Williston Walker, Richard A. Norris, David W. Lotz, and Robert T. Handy, *A History of the Christian Church*, Fourth Edition (New York: Scribner's Reference, 1985), 25.

9. Marshall, 153.

10. See William A. Smalley, "Cultural Implications of an Indigenous Church," in *Practical Anthropology*, vol. 5 (New Caanan, Conn.: New Caanan Publishing, 1958), 54.

11. Ibid.

4. Hang Out and Hover: An Indigenous Satellite Strategy

1. J V Thomas, *Investing in Eternity, The Indigenous Satellite Church Strategy* (Dallas, 1991).

Notes

2. Charles Lee Williamson, *Growing Your Church in Seven Days* (Dallas: Creative Church Consultations, 1994).

3. The 1974 survey was given in a report to the state missions commission of the Baptist General Convention of Texas by J V Thomas.

4. J V Thomas, "The Church and the Poor." A paper prepared for The Nature of Human Nature: A Study of Motivation MLA 6361, A. Q. Sartain, Professor (Southern Methodist University, Dallas, Texas, 1974).

5. The authors' notes from a Baptist General Convention of Texas, Church Extension Conference (March 1973) Dallas, Texas.

5. A Multihousing Strategy

1. Notes from J V Thomas, Church Extension Section Coordinator, B.G.C.T. in instructions from Charles Lee Williamson, Missions Division Director, State Missions Commission, Baptist General Convention of Texas, Dallas, Texas.

2. Verbal report from Harvey Kneisel, Director of Missions Corpus Christi Texas Association.

3. See Joe Klein, "In God They Trust," *New Yorker Magazine*, 16 June 1997, 47.

4. Ibid., 48.

5. Dr. Milfred Minatrea. A strategic document prepared for the Dallas Baptist Association Mega Focus Cities Report, Priority Four: Multihousing (June 1, 1993), p. 4-a.

6. The Ahlens live in a multihousing community in the Oak Cliff section of Dallas.

7. George Hunter, *How to Reach Secular People* (Nashville: Abingdon Press, 1992), 44-53.

8. Beal, *Opening Doors* (Atlanta: Home Mission Board, SBC, 1973), 7.

9. Hunter, 79.

10. Toby Frost, *Special Evangelistic Events* (Alpharetta, Ga.: North American Mission Board, 1997).

Appendix 1

1. The definition of the church will be determined by the denominational tradition of the sponsor. Be sure your definition fits into your denomination's teaching. How you define the nature of the mission congregation is critical to its future relationship with the denomination.

2. Most denominations have a creed or confession of faith that guides local churches on doctrinal issues. A simple reference to that document will suffice.

3. In denominations where pastors are appointed by regional judicatories, bishops or superintendents, rather than by a congregational call, this procedure will need to be adjusted substantially.

Appendix 2

1. From Leon McBeth at the First Baptist Church of Dallas.